arning
money after
you've retired

Earning
money after
you've retired

Inspirational ideas to supplement
your pension

Rosie Staal

Editor: Roni Jay

new tricks for old dogs

Published by White Ladder Press Ltd

Great Ambrook, Near Ipplepen, Devon TQ12 5UL

01803 813343

www.whiteladderpress.com

First published in Great Britain in 2007

10 9 8 7 6 5 4 3 2 1

13-digit isbn 978 1 905410 22 4

British Library Cataloguing in Publication Data

A CIP record for th

Designed and typese
Cover design by Julie
Printed and bound by TJ International Ltd, Padstow, Cornwall
Cover printed by St Austell Printing Company
With thanks to our cover models, Julia and Alastair Gunning
Printed on totally chlorine-free paper
The paper used for the text pages of this book is FSC certified.
FSC (The Forest Stewardship Council) is an international
network to promote responsible management of the world's forests.

FSC
Mixed Sources
Product group from well-managed
forests and other controlled sources

Cert no. SGS-COC-2482
www.fsc.org
© 1996 Forest Stewardship Council

White Ladder books are distributed in the UK by Virgin Books

White Ladder Press
Great Ambrook, Near Ipplepen, Devon TQ12 5UL
01803 813343
www.whiteladderpress.com

Contents

Acknowledgements

I am immensely grateful to the dozens of kind people, some known to me, many not, who have made such valuable contributions to this book through their willingness to complete case study questionnaires.

Some have preferred to use a pseudonym yet all of them deserve recognition for the part they have played.

So too do two organisations, The Age and Employment Network and Life Academy, who helped by recruiting some of the case study volunteers from among their membership.

Sincerest thanks also go to Denise O'Leary and Stuart Patterson, supportive friends for whom the call of duty is always exceeded with good humour, and to my husband, David, for his inestimable help and guidance. Finally, I am greatly indebted to Sir Antony Jay for coming up with the idea for this book in the first place.

Chapter 1

In the earning zone

You've done it! You've left work. On the mantelpiece, the 'Happy Retirement' cards evoke that bitter sweet last day when your work colleagues shook you by the hand and confided, 'Wish it was me' and 'Lucky old you', before returning to their familiar daily routine.

They left you to go and start this curious new life which, although you knew it was coming, has been so hard to imagine.

Retirement doesn't come as a surprise, indeed it is a landmark that most will have been anticipating and thinking about for a long time. But now that moment has arrived and it is time to put those long planned ideas, whether vague or detailed, into practice.

So what are you going to do with yourself? The years are, you hope, stretching ahead enticingly – at least 10, probably 20, maybe even 30 or more if you're lucky and if you have your sights set on a congratulatory cyber-message from King William V to mark your 100th birthday.

Your parents, their parents and the generations before them, had no problems envisaging their retirement years. Not a great deal was expected of them and few would have thought of pushing back any of the traditional boundaries. Undemanding years of leisure, relaxation and a certain degree of penury beckoned and then enfolded them.

If there was such a thing as a mortgage – Britain's home-owning culture is a comparatively recent phenomenon – it had long been paid off. Financial concerns extended not far beyond ensuring the surviving spouse could live in reasonable comfort and there was enough put by to cover the cost of a decent funeral.

It's very different now. There are an awful lot more of you, for a start. You are the advance guard of the Baby Boom generation, that first vast wave of post-war babies nourished with cod liver oil and orange juice, now facing retirement on a very different diet.

Boomers may be getting old but they don't seem to grow up. Look at their parents and compare them at the same age: so staid, so sensible, so hidebound by tradition and with such low horizons. Now the outlook for Boomers is quite different, their expectations are far greater and they're looking for far more out of their retirement.

> If you are going to earn some money, to what extent do you want (or even need) to top up your pension and enhance your financial security? Up to what age do you reckon you will need to fund your retirement? Do you think you'll live to be 95? They may all be unanswerable questions but they need to be carefully considered. Everyone has to make their own judgment, which is something that's best done with advice from an expert. There are plenty of independent financial advisers to choose from, so ask around for a recommendation and maybe weigh up the advice you are given from two or three sources before deciding on the course you want to take.

Baby Boomers are probably the last generation of salary related pensioners. They're lucky and they know it, so much so that they're enjoying being fairly adventurous with their money. The Ski set (Ski = Spending the Kids' Inheritance) are a large and potent force in the marketplace. There is a popular philosophy of 'do it now – don't wait', because no one knows how long they're going to be around to enjoy the fun. The next generation is unlikely to be as fortunate and many who are now in their 30s are likely to be still clocking on and drawing a salary at the age of 70-plus.

A survey of 1,770 people aged between 50 and 69 for Heyday, Age Concern's membership organisation, revealed that more than half would like to work on beyond state pension age. Nearly 10% said they didn't want to retire at all. However, nearly two-thirds (64%) said it was impossible to get a new job within 10 years after retirement.

It also found that financial need was the driving force behind 45% of them wanting to work. Some 24% said they didn't have adequate pension savings and a further 21% wanted to continue working because they didn't believe the State Pension would give them enough income in later years.

As older people are living longer, healthier lives, Heyday stresses the need for them to take greater care in planning their financial, social and recreational lives if they are to avoid many of the difficulties being faced today by those in later life.

Financial need at this stage of life is not necessarily prompted by debt, though there is plenty of that about, perhaps caused by a lingering mortgage, an ambitious remortgage or a mid-life divorce. It is more often the case that new retirees want to maintain a lifestyle to which they have become accustomed and those puny pensions won't allow it. Life on a reduced income might have been necessary when starting a family and there was only one salary entering the household, but it can sap the spirits when the situation is stretching ahead indefinitely and retrenchment and parsimony are destined to be a permanent part of that existence.

The Office for National Statistics says that a third of the UK population will be over 50 by 2020. Older people have astonishing economic power in this country. One impressive statistic frequently trotted out is that the over-50s control 80% of the wealth, which totals more than

£240 billion. And they're not spending it all on stairlifts and hearing aids, it seems. They're splashing quite a lot of their cash on facelifts and fitness equipment, health farms, holidays and ... hedonism.

A degree of hedonism, or certainly a completely different way of life, beckons for some people who choose to live abroad when they retire. Possibly as many as four million, or one in five, will have chosen to do this by 2020, according to an Alliance & Leicester Bank study.

Anyone with a holiday home abroad enjoys the flexibility of being able to use it for income or pleasure – or, ideally, both. And if it's in the right area of the right country, it's going to increase in capital value, too, making it a worthwhile asset for any pensioner.

If you don't happen to own a second home abroad, or even if you do, then working on another continent could be within your grasp if you explore the opportunities offered by the Voluntary Service Overseas (VSO). The organisation [**www.vso.org.uk**], which utilises the skills of volunteers in numerous countries around the world, invites applications from people up to the age of 70. Obviously, you wouldn't be paid for what you do, but you could rent out your home while you were abroad and build up a useful nest egg to crack open on your return to the UK.

Some retirees downsize their homes, releasing capital and reducing household bills for the future. It can be a very wise move, provided it is based on a great deal of research and is undertaken willingly and not grudgingly.

Keeping your eyes peeled for earning opportunities can be as rewarding in your sixties as it was when you were 16. Although a paper round may not be up your street (there are many older paperboys and girls who make profitable use of their early rising), hand-written cards in shop windows frequently yield a good variety of jobs ideally suited to an older person. Graduates of the University of Life have a lot to offer advertisers desperately seeking occasional babysitters, gardeners, car cleaners or pub glass washers.

Remember that you grew up alongside space exploration and computer technology, when boundaries were pushed back with impunity, so in keeping with the spirit of your age, you won't be looking to retire *from* anything. Instead, as you leave your company issue gold watch to gather dust on the bedside table, you can happily turn your attention to what it is you would like to retire *to*.

You'll need to have something of the pioneer spirit about you: only 2% of over-65s in the UK are in employment. However, brace yourself for a profound change in the whole work dynamic of this country because we are undergoing a demographic shift of major proportions. Society is getting older every year. By 2012 the number of people in the UK aged over 65 is expected to exceed those under 16, and by 2021 the over-60s will, for the first time, outnumber the twenty- and thirty-somethings. Bring on the reshaped retirement!

Chapter 2

Motivations (and barriers) to work

While you are contemplating exactly what to do to earn money and how you're going to go about doing it, you would be well advised to make a list of reasons. It could be useful not only to get you started but also to refer to again in the future, perhaps if you are going through an uncertain phase and you question what prompted you into action.

As well as the fairly obvious financial motivation, your list is likely to feature some or all of these other reasons for wanting to work:

- **To have a structure to your life**

  There is no denying the fact that once the novelty of retirement has worn off, the empty days can blur into a shapeless, grey nothingness. With a reason to get out and be somewhere by a certain time, on a regular basis, you are able to build a solid framework for your new existence. And remember: the more you have to do, the more you get done.

- **To maintain contact**

  It's important not to feel marginalised and look at life from the sidelines. You will want to keep in touch with the outside world and be aware of what's going on beyond your four walls, so to avoid that cast adrift feeling, some kind of work activity is a great idea. It also helps put your own life and minor niggles into context when you are made aware of others' concerns.

- **To keep physically and mentally active**

  You can't beat moving about – and giving the brain a regular workout. For feeling good about yourself and, hopefully, for helping to stave off all sorts of darkly threatening nasties that lurk around the edges of the lives of those of middle years and older, activity for body and mind needs to be high on the agenda. Put simply, all these will feel the benefit: eyesight, hearing, appetite, blood pressure, agility, flexibility, good humour, dexterity, heart – so it could be just what the doctor ordered.

- **To maintain an identity**

  Just because you no longer have the job title that you earned over so many years doesn't mean to say you can't be an interesting person in your own right. Knock 'em sideways at tedious parties when people who know you're retired think you'll only want to talk about daytime TV. How pleasing to be able to tell them about how you're earning money nowadays.

- **To achieve self-esteem**

  New skills learnt in a new environment will give you such a boost. Simply knowing you are doing something not just for yourself but that affects others' lives for the better will raise your standing. Self-esteem can't help but grow when you stop taking the line of least resistance and find you can do things you might not have thought possible.

- **To feel part of a team**

  There's an unmistakeable fuzzy feeling when you know that others rely on you and you perform well and don't let them down. Pulling together, working for a common cause, being mutually reliant – all these factors link up to make certain types of work very alluring.

- **To have a social network**

  Friends and contacts invariably come through your place of work, wherever and whatever it is. But perhaps more importantly at your stage of life, any sort of job post-retirement can help you keep in touch with news, lifestyle trends, fashions, what's hot and what's not – all the little things that make the world go round and which could otherwise easily pass you by and leave you isolated as a social dinosaur. Perish the thought.

- **To fulfil a need to contribute**

  So many people of retirement age say they want to put something back into the community. This is both laudable and understandable, for after years of a life led quite probably at a headlong dash there is at last time to slow down and consider where best your talents and energies can be directed to benefit others. The 'need' perhaps springs from a highly developed social conscience, something that afflicts a lot of people as they get older – thank goodness.

- **To put to good use the practical skills and life skills, knowledge, experience and wisdom gained over the years**

  Being in your third age (a rather coy expression which is in wide usage so you will have to get used to it) you have so much to offer – and fortunately there is a market for it all. Gather together your great resources and lay them out for employers to see. You should have some pleasant surprises, but no more than they will.

  Personal fulfilment is an important by-product of planning and securing work post-retirement. You can have the great satisfaction of knowing you are making a difference at a time of life when you may have felt that you were, if not worthless, then certainly a little less valuable to mankind than before. Now you'll be listened to, sought out for your experience and opinions, made to feel part of a team and recognised for your achievements.

Why on earth should you want to earn money after you've retired? Why shouldn't you just sit and put your feet up, admire your new slippers and wait for Time's wingèd chariot to gallop over the horizon and pull up by your armchair so you can climb aboard?

Leave that to the others. Hanging about in God's waiting room holds little appeal. So, if you're up for it, push back the armchair, kick off the slippers and get on and do something with your time and your talents.

Hard work and routine may have ruled your life for the past few decades but you can't just turn it off like a tap. We've all heard the sad story of the man or woman who, within a year of saying farewell on their retirement day is taking centre stage again among their old colleagues – but this time at their own funeral. In between the two events they have done little with their lives except wake up to days stripped of their structure and purpose.

Factors to bear in mind in your deliberations about earning money include the three constituent parts of retirement. These are:

- **The Good:** *you have more time, you have at last got your life back, there's the opportunity to travel, there's less stress*

- **The Bad:** *money – there's suddenly a lot less of it than there used to be; health – it could be the one thing that lets you down*

- **The Ugly:** *Your age, lack of drive, lack of money, social isolation, boredom, lack of independence*

There are of course some people who, as they approach retirement, are merely bursting to do nothing at all with their time. No dreams, no fantasies, no unfulfilled ambitions have propelled them through their final working days. If they have no interests outside of work either, then they and, God help them, their spouse, face years of emptiness and atrophy. But maybe they like it that way. Maybe they feel that after years of work they should now be rewarded by entering a state of vacuum.

At least they will be protected there from many of life's harder knocks, such as those that come from continuing brushes with the uglier side of work, commerce, taxation and bitchy colleagues. However, if they need to earn money once they've retired, then they'll have to get out of that vacuum and get a life.

> Research carried out for financial services provider JPMorgan Invest reveals that only about one in seven (14%) workers can look forward to a comfortable retirement. Nearly two-thirds (64%) are facing a 'difficult' retirement, defined as a pension of 40% or less of final salary (weighted against the cost of living).
>
> The situation is particularly worrying for women, where three-quarters (74%) are heading for a difficult retirement compared with a little over half (55%) in the case of men. For women aged 55-59 this rises to 93%. For women in the 25-34 age range the figure is only 57%. The improvement for younger women is probably a reflection of the rise in retirement age, the increasing earning capacity of women generally and the longer time available to come to terms with the increase in life expectancy.

What's going to stop you earning money in some way or other once you've retired? Here are some of the barriers.

1 All those things just waiting to be done.

i Golf – for a great many people retirement means either more time to play golf or the longed for opportunity to take up the game. Either way, it means hours spent out of doors undoubtedly enjoying yourself – but not earning any money.

ii That pile of books you're longing to read – let it build up so that one day, when you're really old and really tired, you'll be glad of the diversion.

iii All those DIY jobs that have been put off until now – the bathroom you want to update or the old chair you want to upholster. Think how much more fulfilled you will feel when you achieve those things and take on a part-time job as well. Multitasking is key.

2 Charity work

This is almost inextricably linked with retirement. So many charities are reliant on older people's usefulness and availability that they face huge difficulties as the pool of talent diminishes. This is mainly because fewer people are offering to work for nothing until they are in their 70s as the over-60s are too busy after retirement. It troubles your conscience, doesn't it, because retirement means it's time for voluntary work? No harm in mixing charity and paid work – many do, and they swear by it. Again, if you're multi-skilled (and by definition of your age you must be – surely) then you can multitask.

3 Grandparenting

Forgive me, but isn't the great thing about having grandchildren the fact that you can hand them back? So why do so many grandparents keep such a firm hold that they saddle themselves with caring responsibilities to the detriment of their own lives? By all means be involved in babysitting but beware of becoming what amounts to a single mother, or father – and all the lack of freedom and the isolation that that involves. Be selfish: you've earned your space and time, so don't surrender it without very carefully thinking through the consequences. Bear in mind that undertaking daytime childcare could result in your having less freedom than when you were working. The key to this one is learning when to say No.

4 The age thing

This is the big one. There are many upsetting stories of older people whose 100 job applications all came to nothing because, they suspect, they were overqualified or over the hill – or both – in the eyes of their prospective employer. Equally, there are heartening tales of others who have almost had their hands snatched off by firms eager to have someone with maturity and valuable life skills on their side. But this is about age as a barrier.

The Employment Equality (Age) Regulations that came into force in October 2006 make it unlawful to discriminate against workers under the age of 65 on the grounds of age.

Part of the point of the new legislation is to counter the ageist attitudes of some employers but in tightening up the language of recruitment, some say it has opened up almost more opportunities for discrimination than it has closed.

This is particularly so in the case of over-65s, for whom the regulations bring an abrupt curtain down on their working life because 65 is now the default retirement age (DRA), the age at which an employer can retire someone without the need to justify it providing they follow the statutory 'retirement process'. Employers may also refuse to recruit anyone over the age of 65.

An amendment to the legislation that would give over-65s the same protection from discrimination that younger workers have is being sought by Heyday, the arm of Age Concern that helps people prepare for and make the most of retirement. Heyday is pursuing its case to the top and has got the case swiftly referred from the High Court to the European Court of Justice from where a definitive ruling is likely to be made during 2008.

It has consulted more than 60,000 Baby Boomers on a range of issues including work and retirement and found that 80% believe there should be no forced retirement, and 65% plan to work past pension age of 65 for men and 60 for women (due to rise to 65 by 2020).

Ailsa Ogilvie, Director of Heyday, says: "The prompt reference to the ECJ means that we will achieve the earliest possible resolution on behalf of the tens of thousands of workers who are forced into retirement each year.

"The UK was one of the last countries in Europe to enact the European directive outlawing age discrimination in employment – and we believe the Government got it wrong.

"For the many people who have been victims of pension changes, who don't have a decent pension or who need to continue earning money after 65 for whatever reason, the right to work free from discrimination is not an optional extra, it's something they need."

The Employment Equality (Age) Regulations are but a first step along a very long road towards changing attitudes towards age in the workplace. As Rachel Krys, of the Employers Forum on Age, says: "We've had legislation in place for 30 years that outlaws discrimination on grounds of gender or race and now we are embarking on this root and branch change in attitude towards age. But the reality is that we are only as good as our weakest link."

Influences such as cultural and demographic shifts have had an effect on attitudes to ageism, and now that these Regulations are in place (pending a review in 2011) it should at least be possible to bring into line those employers who suffer from entrenched attitudes. The DRA, however, could be seen to play straight into their hands because they are the very people whose inflexibility provided the argument against a default retirement age.

Rachel Krys adds: "It has helped but it is not the panacea. There are quite a few years of frustration ahead."

The bottom line of these new Regulations is that they should make life easier for over-50s who are working as their age is made irrelevant. But once you reach 65, in other words you attain what is now the DRA, the Regulations say you have no right to remain in work and merely have the right to request an extension of your working life. For an employer to 'retire' you they have to prove it is 'objectively justified'.

Professor Stephen McNair, director of the Centre for Research into the Older Workforce (Crow) at Surrey University, says the UK has a long way to go even to retain people in work until pension age. On average, British workers retire at 62.1 years – men at 63.1 and women at 61. This is one of the highest average retirement ages in the EU yet is still well below the official pension age.

Prof McNair says his centre's research has shown that people do want to go on working but not full time. "People in general feel positive about work. If employers design work in appropriate ways, with flexible and part-time options, they can keep an older workforce," he says.

Crow has compiled this list of older workers' attributes:

- Conscientiousness
- Job effectiveness
- The ability to think before acting
- Loyalty
- Less absenteeism
- Interpersonal skills
- Team working

Even with all these attributes, the odds are heavily stacked against older people and it isn't always possible to pop up from nowhere and snatch a slice of whatever you fancy. Shoulder charging closed doors – or, put another way, making multiple job applications and being persistent – could be an unwelcome post-retirement pastime for some.

To illustrate how irksome rules and regs can be, how they don't favour older people and how dogged your attitude must be in your search for work, Bryan, who is 68, tells his story.

Most of my life I was a professional engineer/physicist working for the Central Electricity Generating Board until privatisation, when my part of the industry continued under state ownership as Nuclear Electric until that too was privatised in 1994.

I retrained and qualified as a teacher but found it impossible for someone of my age (then 57) to find employment in any school and so I began to look at the Further Education sector. Even there I was told that I would find it very difficult to get a full time post and that most people entering the profession at my age would probably only be able to get part-time work at low rates of pay.

Luckily, I did secure a position as a full time lecturer in Information Technology at a local College. The Principal in those days was actually keen to employ people who had industrial experience, so perhaps this counted in my favour.

I believe I was good at teaching and had five successful years during which I like to think I brought some useful benefit both to my students and to the College.

But then I began to suffer from extreme exhaustion which at the time I considered to be due to long working hours coupled with conditions of considerable stress associated with teaching 16-19 year olds in an FE College. I was also trying to deal with the constantly changing requirements placed on Colleges at that time.

My performance began to deteriorate as a result and a year later, aged 63, I felt I could no longer continue working with the teenagers, but I continued to work for the College doing mostly adult classes on a part time basis right up to my 65th birthday.

In fact, it wasn't long after giving up my full-time post that I was diagnosed as having a heart arrhythmia, which was successfully treated with a pacemaker.

I believe that the development of this condition may also have been responsible for the dip in performance which had caused me to have to give up my full-time position, but of course this wasn't realised at the time.

Since having the pacemaker my health has returned to its former good state but by now I was well and truly in the shadow of the age at which I would become effectively unemployable and it proved impossible for me to regain a substantive post despite all my qualifications, knowledge and experience.

I continued to work part-time at the College but after the first year a new Principal, who seems to be resolutely set against employing older workers, arrived and I was only given a very small amount of work (two hours a week).

I approached another College which was able to offer me considerably more work, but still only on short fixed term contracts. When I reached 65, the Principal at the first College sent me a message to say that I would not be offered any further work because of my age.

She apparently didn't feel that she should have spoken to me and indeed when I asked for a meeting with her to discuss possible alternatives, she refused on the grounds that she was bound to follow College policies and couldn't change her decision. Fortunately for me, the second College was quite happy for me to continue after the age of 65, still on short fixed term contracts. However, due to funding cuts and poor enrolments in IT, they were unable to offer me any further work as a part-time teacher, and could only offer me work as a support worker/learning mentor.

Part-time teachers are paid around £20 per hour while support workers/learning mentors only attract around £10 an hour. I accepted some of this work and am still doing that now. In fact, because of the shortage of work in IT, I have been taking courses myself in order to equip me to work in the Skills for Life field (Adult Literacy and Numeracy support) and will now be looking for work in that area as well. However, initial impressions are that, despite all the money the Government are pouring in to this area at the expense of general adult education, there isn't much response from the public, and therefore not many jobs are available at the moment.

I have worked hard all my life and I think I have achieved some useful things during that time. Working, especially helping others to achieve their goals, is something which is part of my life and will always be so as long as I am fit and well enough to go on doing it.

However, I am very disappointed to say that FE Colleges generally will not employ anyone over the age of 65 in a substantive post. This is, of course, a product of their adoption of Mandatory Retirement Ages. Non-recruitment of older workers goes hand in hand with that. Some Colleges are willing to employ older people on short fixed term contracts while others operate a complete ban on allowing such people to even apply for advertised posts. This is, of course, not illegal, even under the new regulations, but it is definitely age discrimination in a thin disguise.

I feel greatly frustrated that I could do so much more if only my age didn't act as a barrier, not in my eyes, but definitely in the eyes of many other people. This has not been helped by the new Age Regulations since they themselves discriminate against people who are over the age of 65. Before there was a default retirement age employers often used to be a little coy about practising age discrimination in the form of compulsory retirement, although they still did it. Now though, they feel quite confident that they can do it with impunity.

The job application forms for one College I have recently applied to says that "all applicants will be treated equally regardless of age, disability, ethnic origin, gender, marital status, religion, sexual orientation, offending background etc.", which is, of course, very commendable, but when I enquired if the College was still operating a mandatory retirement age they said:

"The College has a default retirement age of 65 in line with recent Age Discrimination legislation. Staff can request to work beyond this age if they wish, however permission for this would only usually be granted if there was a legitimate business need to justify it."

This, of course, means that they won't consider recruiting anyone over the age of 65 (or even possibly 55 or 60) giving a lie to their statement about equal treatment regardless of age, etc.

This is fairly typical of the double speak which surrounds this subject. Other examples can be found in the Age Regulations themselves and these are what has prompted the action, on behalf of people like myself, taken against the Government by Heyday.

I love working, especially using the skills I have accumulated to help others. I value the regular voluntary work I do just as highly, if not more, than the work for which I receive a small amount of pay (about £190 a week gross).

Having been a lifelong worker, to coin a phrase, and a lifelong union member, working for low pay is something which does rankle from time to time since I sometimes have the uncomfortable feeling that I am somehow being taken advantage of. The voluntary work is, of course, done for expenses only and is therefore free from such feelings, but they both give me a huge amount of job satisfaction accompanied by the feeling that I am still able to make a useful contribution.

Chapter 3

Going it alone

STARTING YOUR OWN BUSINESS

Being your own boss is an attractive proposition if you have a good idea you want to put into practice or you can't bear the thought of working for anyone else. A working life spent in the sort of corporate environment that breeds antipathy can have a beneficial spin-off: you will look for absolutely anything that avoids replicating that sort of existence. So if toeing the company line is no longer your thing, then maybe it will have given you the impetus you need to propel you into a new and more exciting way of work, away from all the horrors that go hand in hand with cut and thrust corporate life in the 21st century.

Perhaps you have become bored with working in one particular area of business and you are anxious to branch out into something different. Whatever the reason, you must view your next move with a great deal of realism.

Just because you think you've got a great idea and it's something you'd like to do, it doesn't mean to say that it would be realistic in practice. Beware the realms of fantasy and beware the desire to run your own show because you want control over your life.

You may have spent years working under pressure for a dreadful manager and now you see an opportunity to run your own scene. Don't be hasty. You've worked for difficult managers, just wait until you've got difficult customers. You haven't seen anything until you're dealing with an angry client – particularly if their complaint is completely unjustified.

Do bear in mind that if you start out on your own you've got to be your own human resources manager, your own lawyer, your own health and safety manager, facilities manager, logistics manager, networker – the whole shebang.

If you are unsure about the level of your motivation, see if you react with an enthusiastic 'Yes please, I'll have some of that' to all of these spin-offs of running your own business or being self-employed:

- As the boss, you are in control of your working future
- No more company politics or corporate environment
- Experiencing the satisfaction of seeing something grow that you have created for yourself
- Independence, enjoyment and fun
- You would organise how, when and where to work
- Experiencing the thrill of taking calculated risks
- Having a marketable and viable product or service
- Being in a position of authority
- Having the opportunity to earn a substantial amount of money

No longer answerable to others, now is the time for you to be in charge and call the shots. You will be responsible for what you do and nobody else – a great feeling for all those heartily fed up with accommodating other people's foibles and shortcomings. But before you race off to order the business cards, take time to research every aspect of your idea. Many careers advisers do their best to put people off solo business start-ups. Most fail within the first year, so be warned.

"I always try and talk people out of it," says Simon, a career transition consultant. "And if I don't manage to do it, then they usually do it for themselves once they've worked on a business plan. That's the clincher, if income is crucial. I work very hard to make people see the reality."

The importance of spending time and trouble on a business plan cannot be overemphasised. It isn't just for the benefit of the bank manager, it is for your own peace of mind and so you can see if your idea has legs and will one day make you some money. If you have no business plan then you have no business.

One retiree who Simon was helping was single-minded about setting up as a dog walker. He had a friend who was doing it in the next town and really fancied the idea himself, not least because the friend seemed to be making such a good go of it.

Simon's insistence that he should prepare a business plan meant the facts ended up telling a different story and his client's hopes of a business based on taking other people's housebound dogs for regular walks were soon dashed. The would-be entrepreneur found that far from it being the reasonably relaxed way of making money that he had expected, his plan showed he would have to work eight hours a day every day of the year, to achieve anything like the sort of income he needed. Back to the drawing board.

So, along with a business plan and some more realistic ambitions, what else do you need if you are going to succeed in business? Here are some prerequisites:

- Your own job description (which you must be prepared to rewrite at regular intervals)
- An honest evaluation of your strengths and weaknesses and your suitability for the 'job'

- An utter belief in your business idea and a burning desire to make it profitable

- An ability to organise yourself and your time effectively and efficiently

- A sharp awareness of any competition and the viability of your business in the marketplace

- A willingness to network and develop opportunities and business relationships

- An ability to demonstrate flair, creativity, stamina, patience, motivation and enthusiasm

- An ability to cope with disappointment and not crumble in the face of setbacks

- A willingness to take risks if necessary

- Good communication skills

- Financial wisdom

- A willingness to acquire news skills and knowledge

- Competence with computers and familiarity with the internet

- An ability to manage change and uncertainty in a constantly fluctuating environment

Inevitably, there are many other considerations before you launch yourself on the waiting world. If you are fortunate enough to have been able to satisfy all the 'needs' listed above, then you might yet be tripped up by some of those that involve people close to you. For instance, you will have to take into account the support – or, to be realistic, possible lack of support – that might be forthcoming from family members.

Have you canvassed their views about your idea? Can they, will they, help you? What form will this help take and can you, honestly, rely on it? Generous promises of support that fizzle out after the first week or at the first sign of pressure could be disastrous and you really need to be sure that any commitment is genuine and not just being said to flatter, encourage or humour you.

Will the family continue to be supportive once they find that your business is encroaching on their time and, perhaps, their space in the home? They need to be aware of all the implications before you can hope for them to be on your side. The last thing you want is for your business to be scuppered by unsupportive family members who resent the fact they were never told how much it would affect them.

Equally, be honest with the family about any financial implications. Secretly ploughing your mother-in-law's legacy into your self-employment fantasy isn't a good move if you value marital harmony. Set out all the finances clearly and fairly and discuss them with those who have a right to know.

Among the cautionary tales of those who didn't is the sad story of Nigel, who overlooked the need to spell out his financial situation to his wife and nearly got himself kicked out of the family home. He cashed an insurance policy to help cover the costs of setting up as a driving instructor but failed to tell his wife. When she retired two years later and started planning the holiday of a lifetime that they'd always promised themselves, she discovered that there was no insurance policy to fund the dream.

Nigel acknowledges that two months spent sleeping on the sofa was a fair price to pay for such thoughtlessness on his part.

There is a fundamental need for you to ensure that your venture is taken seriously by the family. It is not a 'little job', it is your new business and it is going to be a big part of your life. Sharing its importance with the family will help underline its significance and ensure they are on your side through the bad times and the good.

[A good first stop for advice is **www.primeinitiative.org.uk** which is specifically to help over-50s set up in business, or find inspiration and information at **www.startups.co.uk**.]

Among the aims you set yourself, make sure that at the top of the list 'enjoyment' is alongside 'an excess of income over expenditure'. After that, the order of the list doesn't really matter.

PROS:

- You decide how much you want to invest – financially and time-wise
- You can aim as low or as high as you wish
- Exploiting some of the many sources of advice, funding and subsidies
- Profits after tax are all yours
- No one is going to interfere with the way you choose to run your business
- Once your business is up and running you could sell, franchise or float it on the stock market
- An unmatchable sense of achievement
- Being challenged and stretched at a time when you could just atrophy
- The pleasure of thinking, or even saying, 'I told you I could make it work'

CONS:

- Being one of the majority of business start-ups that fail in their first year
- Having to tackle a steep learning curve at a time when it all seems such an effort
- Suffering regular pressure and knock-backs

- Having to suffer the ignominy of others saying 'I told you it wouldn't work'

Learn how others have fared – and learn from their experiences, too. Here are the stories of five people who have launched themselves into business after retirement with varying degrees of effort and who are, happily, still able to smile about it. As with all the case studies in the book, ask yourself when reading it: 'Could I do this, or something like it?'

The managing director

Frank, 76, formerly a Police Chief Superintendent

Why are you still working?

Because you retire relatively early in the Police, you still have plenty left in the tank and certainly in my case I wasn't inclined to sit around doing nothing. My objective was to retain enough independence to enable me to choose whether I worked or not and when and where it suited me. My incentive was to maintain my standard of living by making up the balance over my pension. My expectations have been exceeded in both income and job satisfaction.

What are you doing?

In partnership with my wife I formed a business which we called Executive Services, offering services within my expertise, ranging from management, administration, personnel (or human resources, as it is stupidly called these days), a general fixer or in some cases stopgap to meet a temporary need due to demands exceeding normal resources.

Projects have included fundraising, organising and promotion of events, including fashion shows, concerts, etc; graduates' personnel interviewing and selection for commercial concerns and Civil

Service Commissioners; attending briefings and briefing barristers on behalf of solicitors; planning inquiries; national survey of a company's premises; consultancy for charitable and public affairs; clerk to the mayoralty – and probably quite a lot more over a period of 15 years.

I suppose it could have failed or not come up to expectations but that was not the case – perhaps I was lucky. I like to think that the skills and experience of my previous training had instilled a discipline of method and practice that was appreciated in other fields.

How did it come about?

Having previously worked at the top of a large organisation I resolved that it would be tiresome to try and work for anyone else. I therefore had no choice but to work for myself.

Is it working out well for you?

I worked as 'Executive Services' for 15 years and then for the past seven or so years I have managed my wife's business [the singer Rosemary Squires] on a *quid pro quo* basis – she cooks my meals, washes and darns my socks and I'm her roadie and do her books. It's good. I'm a lucky man.

And the money?

I earned money on the principle that the labourer is worthy of his hire. Yet sometimes on the Robin Hood principle that if I thought it a worthy and interesting endeavour, then I would do it whatever the money – within reason, of course. It helped to know that there was always the pension cheque to fall back on should all else fail.

We are not and did not aim to become rich – we simply sought freedom from anxiety and the means to indulge an occasional extravagance.

To someone like me from a background of establishment and institutional security with a monthly salary cheque, it is essential to get a good accountant to set you on a business footing. Not necessarily one of the major firms that charge an arm and a leg but perhaps someone qualified (who must be qualified to be accepted by, for example, the Inland Revenue) who could be just like me: also retired and earning money to supplement a pension.

PROS:

• Doing something so different from the 'proper' job

CONS:

• None really. It sometimes means antisocial hours but the bonus is having something interesting to do that is a matter of choice, so it's not a problem

The gîtes owner

Daff, 61, formerly a journalist, freelance copy editor and TEFL lecturer

Why are you still working?

Primarily for financial reasons but also as a project to keep fit and active. That way, hopefully, there's no time to get too introspective or ill. Someone once said that you should aim to die when in the middle of planning your next project.

What are you doing?

I live in France with my husband [a retired systems analyst and interactive web specialist] where we have five properties and a ruin which we are restoring. The small cottages are in use as gîtes, so our 'work' is running those, with a considerable amount of effort expended on marketing and on the website. These are important aspects because we deal with customers direct and it's vital to keep the website up in the search engines. This side of the business involves about eight hours a week throughout the year.

Maintenance is also vital, of course, as and when it arises, and probably amounts to about a week of work in any year for the established gîtes.

Admin work accounts for an average of two to three hours a week, with most of it concentrated in the period between February and June.

In the summer, the pace accelerates to 12 hours a week handling changeovers and laundering bed linen (grrr) and being nice to the guests.

The rest of our time we work on the largest house which, once completed, will be ours to live in and not for hiring out.

How did it come about?

By chance. The two first cottages we bought belonged to friends. We had helped them organise finance, and the four of us started letting to pay the interest. That was in about 1998.

We discovered we enjoyed the business. By the time our friends decided to give up it was obvious to us that we would have to do something in lieu of pensions when we retired. So while we were still living in England we bought them out and subsequently bought three more semi-ruins nearby. This all happened before the French property boom, or we couldn't have done it.

Is it working out well for you?

Yes. We are now living here permanently, with a fine supply of interesting people to talk to and no problems about what to do with our time. I get a bit overwhelmed by all the work from time to time, but not in a serious way. We have no TV but we do have broadband and, through Skype, cheap phone links, so can keep in touch with the UK.

And the money?

The holiday lets bring in about a third of our total income at present. The rest comes from my state pension, letting our house in the UK and some investments. It is essential until my husband gets his pension and work-related pension at 65. We don't see ourselves continuing to let all the gîtes after that, but will probably still keep two.

We don't have a problem with the idea of paying tax, and if you start off from that position it is pretty straightforward. Even moving into the French system is looking OK at the moment, though we are using a dual nationality accountant who really knows the ins and outs.

PROS:

- We enjoy setting up good holidays for people
- It is extremely satisfying, even if the day-to-day stuff is tedious
- Without the gîtes we couldn't do the restoration of our house, which is the real joy
- We've made a few real friends for life over the years, and many interesting acquaintances. Generally we see people at their best

CONS:

- I can't think of any, except having to be polite and smiley ALL the time even when we're very tired from building work
- Of course, laundering bed linen
- It's a bit of a pain not being free agents in the summer. We really have to be here most of the time between April and October, although we do have a backstop if we do manage to get away
- We're always expecting the holiday market to disappear as everyone says it's going to, but so far so good

The shop owner

Tom, 62, formerly a swimming pool installer in Spain

Why are you still working?

I was bored and needed something to stop me from climbing up the walls. My wife and I lived in Spain for 18 years but we came back to the Midlands three years ago after I had a heart attack because we thought we'd better be near the family and the good old NHS.

After a year recuperating I decided it was time I got on with the rest of my life. I could have retired and bought a set of golf clubs, but that wasn't what I wanted. Unfortunately, I didn't have a clue what I did want – I just knew I had to do something.

What are you doing?

I run a business with my son, Richard. We have a shop in town which sells computers and all the stuff that goes with them. I'm in charge of that while my son runs around delivering and sorting out people's computer problems in their homes – all the more physically demanding stuff. I deal with the customers, which I love.

How did it come about?

My son's marriage broke up soon after we came back from Spain. He fancied a total life change, including a new job, so he and I talked about going into business together.

Lots of people warned us not to. They said we'd fall out – especially over money. Other people gave us the benefit of their business wisdom and, of course, we took advice from the various agencies that help small firms get off the ground. Our local Business Link organisation was really helpful, and even the bank came up trumps with a business loan and a lot of advice.

We chose to sell computers because Richard and I are both a bit geeky about them. We have always fancied ourselves as technical boffins, right back from the early days when we used to spend hours messing about on his Sinclair Spectrum computer.

Is it working out well for you?

It's working really well. I love it – I couldn't be happier. It's given me a new lease of life. There are very few quiet times in the shop so I'm on my feet nearly all day, but this is what I thrive on.

The learning curve has been steep and continues to be steep, but that's fine. I like a challenge. I make sure I keep at least one step ahead of the customers, but even the most demanding ones realise that I can't know absolutely everything. We can usually answer most queries and solve most problems, though.

Richard and I get on fine – in fact, we've not fallen out over anything. From the day we started with this germ of an idea, right through all the months of research and setting up, I'm proud to say we haven't had a cross word.

And the money?

It isn't about the money, to be honest. At least it isn't for me. It's important to Richard so most of it goes to him.

In the first year I didn't take anything out of the business at all, but in the past few months Richard has insisted I take a share, which is about £700 a month. This will increase as the business grows, but my main concern is that Richard should take out of it all that he needs. I'll be grateful for anything that's left over.

PROS:

- Keeping busy and being useful
- Getting out of the house and out from under my wife's feet
- Playing a key role in growing a successful business

- Meeting people
- Something different happens every day

CONS:

- The occasional awkward or unpleasant customer
- Opening up the shop on a cold, wet Monday morning

BUYING A BUSINESS

If you lack inspiration or can't be sure that your great idea for launching a business really is a winner, then you might consider buying an established business.

First things first: you must be completely convinced that you really will be able to make a go of it. There's a world of difference between working for someone else and working for a business that you have bought with your own money – and it isn't just the financial aspect. There's the physical and mental stress and effort, the emotional commitment and the sacrifice of time and freedom.

Assuming, then, that this isn't a passing whim and that you are sure this is the way forward for you, how do you shape up as a potential purchaser of a business?

Are you:

- Prepared to take on the legacy of the previous owner?
- Aware of every aspect of the business?
- Happy to inherit staff who may resent a new boss?
- Possessed of sufficient talents and strengths to maintain a viable company?

Any new business presents two very obvious challenges: the development of a product or service and the research that will establish how much people will pay for it. Taking on an existing business will ensure that you have a reasonable amount of this sort of information to refer to and on which to base important decisions. The purchase price will include this valuable 'history' along with other such intangibles as goodwill and reputation.

A business with a good track record will make it easier for you to get finance. Once you have found out all you need to know about a business's history, its present status and future potential, you will need to reassess it with you as its nominal boss and see how it measures up.

PROS:

• The business is established

• You may be able to turn to the previous owners for support

• There will be an existing client base

• You could sell the business on

• There is probably a greater chance of success than if you started a similar business from scratch

CONS:

• The investment and business transfer costs are liable to be quite considerable

• A great deal of time and research will be required to identify the best business to buy

The caravan park owner

Steve, 52, formerly a Police Sergeant in the Metropolitan Police Service

Why are you still working?

I didn't retire from life in general when I retired from the Met. My police pension is good but insufficient to live on, so I'm working to keep occupied and to augment my pension.

What are you doing?

My wife and I run a touring caravan park on the edge of the New Forest in Hampshire, which we bought on my retirement.

How did it come about?

We were on holiday in Egypt and made friends with a lady travelling with her granddaughter. Beside the pool one day the lady asked me what I was going to do when I left the police service. I said I was looking for a camping/caravanning site on the south coast, to which she replied: "I have a friend in Ringwood who may be willing to sell." The friend was a member of her over-60s keep fit class and at 78 thought that it was time to retire.

After returning home, a week later she telephoned me and 18 months later it became a reality.

Is it working out well for you?

They say that being self-employed you only work half a day: the other 12 hours you can do anything you want! Susan and I work a 15-hour day seven days a week for the six months that we are open. We are not really rewarded for the hours we work or for the responsibility and we are very restricted by the cleaning schedule and the need to be here to greet new arrivals, to answer enquiries and to maintain security. Our main fear is that strangers will walk on to the site and steal from caravans and awnings or take caravans. The other fear is that travellers may break in when the site is empty or just drive in and refuse to leave. We are fortunate that we experience very little trouble but it is going on at other sites around us.

Susan is responsible for the administration and banking and help-ing with the cleaning of the shower block, which everyone compli-ments us on – even a nurse who says that the immaculate facilities are cleaner than her hospital.

My working day begins at 7.30am when I open the gates, check, and clean if necessary, the toilets and showers, and empty the dustbins. After breakfast I spend two hours on maintenance work. Between 11am and noon each day Susan and I give the shower block a thor-ough clean. Dustbins are emptied again, more maintenance is done and then it's time for lunch at about 1.30pm. Goodbyes will have been said to those leaving before 11am and pitches are prepared for those arriving from 1pm – a real juggling act with the cleaning.

Toilets and showers are checked again at regular intervals through the afternoon and evening and finally at 10.30pm, when the gates are locked. Our telephone is going much of the time with bookings and enquiries. If the caravanners have any problems they come to our front door as this is the reception point.

Afternoons are spent on further maintenance, mainly grass cutting, until about 4pm. Sometimes the caravanners may not arrive until 10pm if they've been held up by traffic jams, breakdowns or ferry delays from France. As part of customer service we endeavour to help the caravanners on to pitches, with the reversing and the set-ting up, especially as some are in their 80s.

When the park closes for the year that isn't the end of it: there are several more weeks of work. This might involve sowing extensive areas of grass seed, gravelling pitches, pruning conifers and gener-al gardening duties using the two sit-on mowers, a Flymo, a petrol grass cutter, four brush cutters and two chainsaws.

And the money?

Basically, if we didn't have my pension to rely on we couldn't do this. I often say that I could earn more money stacking shelves in Sainsbury's – and it's true. Expenses like electricity and water together with waste disposal have doubled in the past three years (not to mention the hassle with EU regulations that goes with it all).

We use my pension of £12,000 per annum to pay for the essentials like rates, cars and mortgage while the site pays for the housekeeping (for the six months we are open) and a holiday. We pay ourselves £5 a day and work for nothing on Sundays.

We have had to adjust from enjoying a joint income of £55,000-plus per annum to less than £18,000 before tax. Our accountant handles the detail of our finances, which is one less job we have to do ourselves.

PROS:

- We have met some really lovely, good and very pleasant people from 'middle England'

- I believe we have surprised ourselves by the amount of work we've undertaken and how we have applied and motivated ourselves to our daily tasks. I've chopped down trees, rebuilt roads, taken apart and rebuilt a kitchen and bathroom, and learnt new skills in plumbing, plastering, carpentry, grass maintenance and using a chainsaw

- I've become a committed recycler: I collect and sort through the rubbish and every two weeks I put out 20 dustbins of recycling, including five bins of glass bottles, three of newspapers and the rest of tin cans and plastic containers. I put it on the kerb where the council collect it for nothing – otherwise I'd have to pay to have so much rubbish taken away

CONS:

- Being here all the time we aren't able to attend family functions or get-togethers with friends for six months at a time

- A few of the regulars here seem to think that I should use my pension to subsidise their lives and incomes

- The location of the park means that deer from the Forest come into our back garden and eat everything (apart from that, it's idyllic!)

- Being caught out by rising costs. One August our electricity bill went up by nearly 80% and we couldn't pass on any of the costs because our pitch charges are fixed for a year at a time. Consequently, we lost £700 for that August and September

- Caravanners who have a knack of arriving as we sit down to lunch

BUYING A FRANCHISE

Most of what has been said about starting up or buying a business applies to an aspiring franchisee. It amounts to taking care and thinking through the whole project thoroughly. At the outset consult The British Franchise Association **[01491 578050 www.british-franchise.org]**, which offers seminars, workshops, forums, exhibitions and professional advice to anyone thinking about investing in a franchise.

Some franchisees part with a lot of money (see Mike's case study, below) for their share of what they have convinced themselves will be a success story. In return, they receive training and support from the franchisor and an ongoing commitment of handholding that brings not just security but peace of mind, too.

Taking on an existing franchise could be a better bet financially than buying one and starting it up from scratch with no existing customers. Again, diligent research [try **www.whichfranchise.com**] will help you choose.

PROS:

- Being a franchisee means you receive continuing support, varying from occasional to 24/7

- If it's under a well known brand name, you won't have to worry about publicity to raise awareness

- You'll be given guidance on any vehicles or equipment required

- Help with promotional and advertising campaigns

- The area in which you work is defined

- The routine 9-5 becomes history

CONS:

- You need a large amount of capital because the costs can mount alarmingly, even after the initial outlay, which could be as low as £1,000

- It may be a little restricting if you fancy yourself as an entrepreneur because you have to follow company policy

The car repairer

Mike, 62, formerly in sales for a chemicals firm

Why are you still working?

We need the money. Unfortunately, we have expensive tastes, especially in holidays, and our combined pensions (my wife was a primary school teacher for 23 years) don't go far enough. Also, I have owned a vintage car – a Jaguar XK140 – for years and I am gradually restoring it to concours condition but it costs a lot of money. I felt guilty spending so much on that and putting so little back into the pot. And finally, I thought work would restore some sort of purpose to my life: tinkering with the Jag is fine, but not all day every day.

What are you doing?

I do minor car body repairs at a customer's home or on the spot where damage has occurred, such as in a car park. I own the franchise for this business and cover a radius of about 35 miles from my home. It's been quite a surprise to find myself as a white van man at my age!

The work is well within my capabilities because of all the years I've spent working on my Jag but also because I've been given good training. Basically, I get a scratched, dented car back to pristine condition. Customers are always amazed at what can be done.

How did it come about?

I was chatting with the guy at my local garage, which specialises in high performance cars and vintage rebuilds – and where I've spent far too much time and money over the years, it must be said. He was telling me about his brother who was running his own car repair franchise business in another part of the country. He was doing really well, apparently. It sounded interesting so I started making inquiries.

In the meantime, while I arranged the finance to buy the franchise (a business loan from my bank) I worked part-time for the garage organising their courtesy car service and helping out with driving or deliveries. That got me back into the work mode again, which was very good for me. I also spent about a month, unpaid, working alongside their valeter, and as he was 74 it gave me confidence that I'd be able to cut it when it came to doing similar work on my own once I'd got my business going.

Is it working out well for you?

The franchisor said I'd be earning from the first day – and he was right. They pass on the leads, so I don't have to go hunting around for custom unless I want to. That was one of the features that appealed to me – after a career in sales I just couldn't face any more knock-backs from the public. It's good because I can take it at my own pace. I will step this up in due course, I expect.

And the money?

The initial investment is quite a lot. I paid £24,000 for the franchise, but for that you get all the training and a very good system of support. On top of that there's a management charge of about £250 a month. It's early days yet – I've only been doing this properly for six months – but I can see how it could develop and, if I wanted, I could grow it and perhaps even take on neighbouring franchises. Maybe I'm a bit long in the tooth for that, but it's interesting to ponder. My plan is that whatever I have spent will prove to be a good investment because not only will I be earning but I will reap a good return when I eventually sell the franchise.

PROS:

- I'm being useful whereas before I was just a drain on our finances

- The work keeps me fit and active

- I get to meet all sorts of people – and I especially like the car obsessed ones

- The time I spend working on my Jag is time that I have carved out in a busy week, so I feel less self-indulgent than before, when I used to tinker from dawn till dusk

- I am pleased to discover how hard I can work, despite advancing years.

CONS:

- I wish I was younger. I'd love to have done this years ago

- Having to get out of bed on the sort of mornings when I'd rather pull the covers over my head

- I don't get enough time to myself

- Dealing with the occasional unpleasant customer
- Thinking this must all come to an end one day when my body gets too creaky for me to carry on

Chapter 4

Working from home

'I work from home.' It sounds so wonderful, doesn't it? It conjures up images of lie-ins, late starts, breakfast when you want it, long lunches, wearing what you like, stretching the hours to fit, taking a day off when you want, finishing the day as early or as late as you like and, best of all, no commuting.

Except the reality is very different. Ask anyone who works from home and they'll tell you that in fact its success stands or falls by your own very determined attitude, no quarter given. And, of course, there is the ever present danger that your friends, knowing you're at home and therefore not busy working, pop in for a chat whenever they wish.

Even if they can't adapt to your schedule, your own self-discipline is the key. Without it, any hopes of making a living through working from home will have about as much chance of success as a seaside donkey in the Grand National. In other words, if you aren't up to it, don't even enter the race.

If you do put in the effort, and you really do resist the urge to lie in when you would rather stay in bed, and you do dress properly to make yourself feel businesslike so you're not slopping about in tracksuit bottoms and a grubby T-shirt, then you have a sporting chance.

Assuming you know what you want to do, and you can truthfully say that the idea complements your strengths and allows for your weaknesses, the next questions to ask yourself are:

- Am I up to it?
- Am I committed enough to the idea?
- Do I have the right attitude?
- Will I be able to keep the momentum going when I haven't got a team around me to give encouragement?
- Would I give myself the job?

As a way of supplementing a pension, working from home has many attractions. It means you can capitalise on your talents and interests but remain in or near the focus of your life. This is especially important if it's difficult for you to get around or you perhaps have caring commitments at home.

As with so many areas of life, scams abound. Some earning opportunities from home (aka homeworking) may be plentiful, but ones that put more money in your pocket than your absent boss may be less easy to find. Beware anything that's described as amazing!!! and incredible!!!! It is probable that you'll be paid less in pounds than the number of exclamation marks in the advertisement.

It is better, if you can, to come up with your own home-based scheme so you remain answerable only to yourself. To help with your plans, it is worth remembering that your home gives you the cheapest office, or studio, that you could ever hope to rent. Dressmaker Jean, for example (see below) works in a sun room at the back of her house, enabling her to take advantage of the best possible light.

> Newly launched initiative WorkerANT is a haven if you are looking to work solo, whether based at home or not. What might have seemed daunting on your own now becomes straightforward and achievable thanks to WorkerANT's internet-based hand-holding. It gives you every chance to enjoy the benefits, flexibility and self-esteem of working inde-

pendently. The website operates on similar lines to internet auction site eBay in that you advertise what you want to sell, which in this case is your particular area of expertise, and compete for jobs posted by would-be employers, who can either buy your service as a fixed package or invite you to tender against other providers.

WorkerANT calls it a "dynamic and self-supporting community" but you could look upon it as your passport to a new way of life. Go to **www.workerant.co.uk**.

SELF-EMPLOYMENT/FREELANCE
The dressmaker

Jean, 79, former secondary and FE teacher of dressmaking and craft

Why are you still working?

I like meeting so many nice people. It also helps me to keep active and occupied and to supplement my income.

What are you doing?

I do dressmaking and alterations for private clients. This can range from taking up a hem on a skirt to making clothes or reconstructing clothing for someone who has put on weight – or lost it. I also undertake commissions, such as painting people's houses on cushions as keepsakes. I used to design knitting patterns but my eyesight isn't good enough for me to do that any more. I teach embroidery, quilting, knitting and fabric painting to a University of the Third Age (U3A) class, but I'm afraid I don't get paid for that.

How did it come about?

I retired from teaching in my late 50s. My husband had been made redundant and we decided to move south to be nearer our daughter. Sadly, my husband died two months after we'd moved so I had some enormous challenges to face. For a long time I was very wobbly but as I got better I began to call on some of the clothing shops in town to see if they needed anyone to do alterations.

All my current work has sprung from those early contacts 20 years ago. At my busiest I was on the books of five shops but gradually they either closed down or stopped using me, so from then on I've just dealt direct with people who either knew me or knew of me.

Is it working out well for you?

It's really good. I can dictate the pace and turn away work if I am too overwhelmed. There seems to be a real need for people with the sort of skills I have. Someone once told me that I was like gold dust. I certainly have a steady flow of work, and it all comes from customers I've had over the years or by word of mouth.

And the money?

I charge £10 an hour. That's the same as I pay the lady who tidies my garden so I suppose it's reasonable, although I think my work requires more skill than hers.

The money has made quite a bit of difference in that I've been able to buy a car for each of my three grandchildren.

It also means I don't have to worry too much about putting my name down for things like outings or Christmas parties with some of the organisations I belong to. If I didn't work I definitely wouldn't be able to do that as I have a very modest basic income.

PROS:

- Keeping busy doing something I enjoy so much
- Being able to do this sort of work from home means I can always make myself comfortable and work in a good light
- My daughter knows where I am – most of the time!

CONS:

- Just the occasional awkward customer who I'd rather not have to deal with, but that's pretty rare
- Working on black material with very small black stitches!

The counsellor and psychotherapist

Anthony, 71, formerly a chef and restaurateur

Why are you still working?

Partly because I retired early, at 54, when I sold my restaurant, partly because I wanted to do something rewarding, and partly for financial reasons.

What are you doing?

I work from home, running a private practice as a counsellor and psychotherapist. It has kept me very busy over the years, but I have recently cut down to two days a week and that's quite enough.

My clients come to me as a result of seeing my entry in the Yellow Pages, via my local professional counselling group or through word of mouth.

How did it come about?

It was my aim to do something entirely different and get out of the treadmill of cooking every day. I was looking out for something that would enable me to give something back to society. It was at the time when both my parents had recently died so maybe it was also as a result of some kind of personal mid-life crisis.

After I closed the restaurant I started thinking about how I used to greet people as they came in to dine. It was so superficial and I decided this would be a worthwhile thing to train to do so that I could meet and get to know people at a deeper level.

Is it working out well for you?

It has worked out very well but it took time to get off the ground – probably two years. The training I did was expensive and it takes time to pay it back.

Training to become a counsellor takes two to three years, part-time, and then you need to be accredited by one of the official bodies, so there are more hoops to go through. Then I did another three years of training in psychotherapy, which goes deeper and is probably more help in the long run.

And the money?

It isn't life-changing; it pays for some holidays.

PROS:

- You can work from home if you have a spare room available
- It's a very interesting job
- Meeting people at a deep level
- No age limit
- Useful to have life experience

CONS:

- You have to be aware that your health can be an issue in that if, for example, you are ill or, as in my case, suffer a slight stroke, you have to cancel patients' appointments and you are therefore in danger of letting down the very people who look to you for reliability and continuity in their lives

The freelance writer

David, 73, formerly an Army officer

Why are you still working?

I don't believe in 'retirement'. Work has always been almost the most important thing in my life and I have no idea of giving it up before it gives me up.

Everywhere you go you see poor wretches who have retired, too early, to a tiny house and garden, leaving themselves nothing left to do but die, which is what they usually do.

Retirement means hell on earth to me – I'd rather wait for hell until I get there.

What are you doing?

I've been working as a freelance journalist since soon after retiring from the Army. I am doing what I feel I was born to do, which is very wonderful.

How did it come about?

It came my way by chance. I always wanted to write. Thirty-plus years in the Army, perhaps surprisingly, was full of writing opportunities of a sort, and I think that I got as far as I did partly because of my expertise in making other, senior, people's thoughts look compelling on paper.

At Sandhurst, one of the beaks (civilian staff – dear old schoolmasters) drew me to one side and said, "You're not ruthless enough to get to the top of the Army, but you have a gift with words – cherish it." I did.

The chance came when my stepdaughter tipped me the wink that one of *Country Life*'s regular diarists was quitting. She was a trainee there, just starting out herself. "Send something in," she said. I did, the only time I have ever sent unsolicited copy, and it took. I wrote that page for 12 years, got noticed, got work, and now have almost as much work as I can handle.

Is it working out well for you?

I have to pinch myself almost daily to believe my luck. I write about life in the countryside – my life and other people's – and about country pursuits. It's all stuff I know about and that is close to my heart.

I work only to commission, but about half the ideas are mine. The work comes in chunks. Often I think it has all died, then suddenly there's an avalanche. I frequently experience long and anxious waits.

I work mainly for *Country Life, The Field* and *Horse & Hound* and review books more or less all the time. I have also published a couple of 'Diary' books, and there's another on the way.

I work for an hour or so a day, sometimes much, much more, but mostly it is comfortable. I have yet to turn down a commission. It's lonely stuff. I write in an attic, but that suits me – I am not gregarious.

I ride every day, virtually live out of doors. It wouldn't do if I was just attic-bound. I've read widely and deeply all my life, and knocked about a bit, all of which gives me the necessary capital to draw on when writing for my principal employers.

And the money?

Current earnings average about £1,000 a month although, like most freelances, I experience periods of feast and famine. Unfortunately, even 30 years in the Army does not prepare you for dealing with people who seldom mean exactly what they say, or have any sense of honour. It's a buyers' market, a great test of editors' character, which many of them signally fail. The exceptions shine in a naughty world and become good friends.

PROS:

- Being self-employed
- Rarely experiencing anything but pleasure and fulfilment in my writing

CONS:

- Working, in some cases, for low grade s***s who would not have been entrusted with a lance corporal's stripe in my regiment, however clever
- Keeping up with the tax situation, having done PAYE all my life

WORKING ONLINE

With high speed, reliable communication being so widely available, many jobs traditionally done in the workplace can now be done perfectly well without having to leave home. There's a rapidly growing number of people beavering away from a spare room or study on projects such as website design and import and export, thanks to computers, Skype phone links, webcams and other essentials of the 21st century teleworker.

And if you're not sure if your idea would bring you the sort of cash you're looking for, keep the example of Steve and Julie Pankhurst in mind: they were the home-based couple who launched Friends Reunited into the ether, and they're never likely to have to worry about topping up their pensions after selling the business for a reputed £120 million.

[For more e-inspiration go to **www.e-grindstone.co.uk**.]

It hardly needs to be said that computer literacy is an absolute must for anyone hopeful of making themselves useful in any way post-retirement, whether financial gain is in mind or not. Just being able to send and receive your family's emails is a bonus, but for job seeking and, increasingly, actual work, computer literacy is more than invaluable – it is imperative.

To acquire the necessary skills, or to brush up those you have, invest time and, where necessary, a little money, in tuition and hopefully the world of work and easy communication should become your oyster. Or at least your whelk.

The online trader

Geoff, 63, formerly a financial adviser

Why are you still working?

Mainly for interest and enjoyment – and it does help to supplement retirement income.

What are you doing?

I have an online trading account to buy and sell stocks and shares. From a hobby it has really developed into a part time job, taking up about two hours a day, or 10 hours a week.

I do a great deal of research, reading the financial press including *The Daily Telegraph* financial pages and the *Investors Chronicle*, visiting various websites and attending company AGMs.

How did it come about?

It has been a hobby for many years and my role as a financial adviser certainly helped.

Is it working out well for you?

It works well for me as I can do it from home and I also help my wife with her savings and financial affairs.

And the money?

In terms of profit, I made about £30,000 last year. It can make quite a difference to the sort of holidays we are able to take. For example we have recently been to South Africa and New Zealand. The money also comes in handy when the drive needs repaving, for example.

I do my own tax return and am currently trying to master the complexities of Capital Gains Tax.

PROS:

- The money
- The interest the activity gives me
- It's enjoyable
- It keeps the mind active
- It keeps me engaged with the economy and what's going on in the world

CONS:

- It can be stressful when the Stock Market crashes

eBay, the online auction site [**www.eBay.co.uk**] has undoubtedly been the catalyst for more people earning from home than anything else in recent years. About 68,000 people in the UK, and 430,000 in the USA, make all or a large proportion of their living through selling items on eBay.

Everyone knows someone who trades on eBay, whether it's as a full-time activity or just for making an occasional purchase or sale. Basically, it is an enormous auction house website, where the world and his wife bid for things they never knew they needed so much – and where transactions are carefully policed to minimise dirty practices. It offers an ideal means of earning an income, from pennies to many pounds, to anyone with access to a computer and the skills to use it.

eBay has spawned stories that have become legends and dreams that have been dashed, but it is a familiar feature in the lives of so many that, used wisely, it can be a really good site on which to base your business, if you have access to items that you are sure will find ready buyers.

The eBay trader

Eve, 67, formerly a secretary in a hospital department

Why are you still working?

I need the money. I was divorced three years ago, as a result of my husband leaving me for a younger model, so I was faced with a financial crisis and the rest of my life rattling round in an empty house.

What are you doing?

I sell vintage items, mostly clothing, on eBay and very occasionally in a friend's shop.

The trading work is about 75% fun mixed with 20% fairly hard work and 5% boring slog. The slog is when I have to wrap parcels and queue at the Post Office with them. The hard work is photographing and listing the items on my eBay site – it's tedious, but at least it uses my intellect because I enjoy writing entertaining descriptions of the pieces to help prospective purchasers get a clear idea of what they might bid for.

The fun is counting the money! It is good fun going off on hunting expeditions: I scour charity shops, car boot sales, white elephant stalls, boxes of junk at auction sales and so on, and nearly always come home with a bundle of things that I know I can turn around for a healthy profit.

I have got to know my market very well now and feel confident that I won't make too many expensive mistakes. My knowledge has increased 20 fold over the two years I've been a serious trader and I'd say that I now have a pretty solid reputation.

How did it come about?

About six months after my husband moved out I managed to pull myself together enough to have a mammoth sort-out of the wardrobes, the attic, everywhere that things had been stored for ages, in what had been our family home for 32 years. I felt like making a fresh start and having a purge of everything that had been around me in my old life.

A friend who helped me kept remarking how lovely some of the stuff was and how it must be worth trying to sell it rather than just chuck it out or send it to a charity shop. There were clothes galore, dating back to the 1960s, because I'm a terrible hoarder, and loads of things like old pictures and household objects that had been moved into our attic when my parents died and their house was sold.

What really decided it for me and made me realise there could be money to be made was when I unearthed my mother's old collection of eggcups. I did a little research and found that some of them, like those from a good studio pottery, or the half-dozen silver art nouveau ones, were worth between £20 and £50 each. It was quite a revelation.

I already had an eBay account because I used to buy a few things, especially DVDs for when the grandchildren came over. I started by listing a couple of my 60s dresses. One of them was a Jean Muir and it fetched an eye-watering amount of money. This encouraged me and soon I was spending every spare minute on building up quite a little business.

Is it working out well for you?

It's great. I wish I'd done it years ago. I had no idea something like this could be so absorbing. It's easy to see how it could take over your life and I have had to force myself to make time for other things as well. I wouldn't want to be an eBay bore, though I could be, quite easily.

And the money?

My income from the trading side is in direct relation to the amount of effort I put in to acquire stock, but I suppose an average month would see me making a profit of about £400. It fluctuates a lot – the summer months are leaner because I take more time away from it, but in winter I'd say the earning possibilities are limited only by the number of hours in the day. There is quite a lot of value in my stock at any time, too, so I am slowly becoming worth a little more.

PROS:

- The money
- It keeps me busy and fills my life with interest
- I've met some great people and made many friends, at auctions and on the internet
- Being much fitter, at last: there isn't much time to take it easy
- Being in charge of my own destiny – that's best of all

CONS:

- Being so reliant on a computer, which has a tendency to be unreliable at the most crucial times

- Dealing with rude customers who I have to be nice to or they might leave me negative feedback on eBay

- Knowing that if I don't buy stock, perhaps if I'm ill for any length of time, then my turnover will nosedive

- Having to wrap parcels nearly every day. It's probably the worst aspect of the work. It takes up a lot of space, too

If you run an online business via eBay you should check if you need to register as self-employed.

HM Revenue & Customs (HMRC) has a guide accessible on its website [0845 915 4515 **www.hmrc.gov.uk**] for online traders. The guide outlines the rules for those who trade online for a profit, as opposed to those selling low value items from home.

HMRC warns that you must be registered if your online activity involves: selling goods that were bought with the intention of reselling them, selling items made yourself for a profit, selling or buying on behalf of others for financial gain or receiving payment for a service.

Anyone running an online business should establish if they need to register for VAT. They may also need to pay income tax, national insurance contributions and fill out a self-assessment return. E-traders starting a new business must let HMRC know within three months of starting trading.

HMRC is said to have a robotic computer software programme that scans internet auction sites looking for people making a large number of transactions.

Chapter 5

A new direction

Striking off down a new path is a very attractive proposition for retirees who want to get out of a rut and take on fresh challenges. A different career can stimulate and excite, bringing interest into an existence that might otherwise threaten to be unremittingly beige.

Stepping off your old straight lines means there are different, wider horizons to head for. Along the way, you could benefit from the refreshing effects that a new experience will bring.

Perhaps you are unsure about taking such a step. It could be that you think you are too old, too vulnerable, too comfortably entrenched in a familiar routine. But think again, because you might surprise yourself. A good dose of courage and a positive attitude could be the making of you and your new career.

If you have always dreamed of doing something different once you've retired, then now is the time to turn into reality all those thoughts and fantasies that sustained you through the rush hour traffic jams or those interminable meetings. Putting out feelers, calling on contacts and networking – all these can help as you seek a way in to your new world of work.

Weigh up your needs and be wary about taking on too much just because the opportunity is there. However, being busy is not the same as being so wall-to-wall preoccupied that you are stressed, as this example illustrates:

A retired senior executive in a financial services company wanted a job in a much smaller organisation where he felt he could make a difference and he wanted to have just a few staff to look after as opposed to several hundred. He was passionate about golf and he got a job as manager of his local golf club, which was about 500 yards away from his home. It was a dream job. Within months he seemed to have taken on quite a lot, what with raising the income of the club and implementing some quite ambitious plans. He seemed really quite burdened. He was also thinking of starting up a business providing IT support to people in their homes.

Friends warned him to be careful in case he reached the stage where he had so much on his plate it would be as though he hadn't retired.

"Don't worry about me," he said. "I'm working very hard, but it's not hard work."

He makes a good point. You can spend from eight in the morning until eight at night out in your garden weeding and pruning and sowing seeds and at the end of it you'll know you've worked very hard but you're not stressed by it at all.

Sounds irresistible, doesn't it?

The tour guide

Annabel, 64, formerly a chartered accountant

Why are you still working?

I like being busy. Also, my husband died suddenly in the year before I finished work at 60 so I had to decide what kind of retirement I wanted as a widow: safe and dull or interesting and useful. By choosing to train for something completely different I have discovered personal strengths that have really surprised me.

What are you doing?

I'm a Blue Badge tour guide, based in London. I'm registered with the London Tourist Board and operate as a freelance. Some of my work comes through personal recommendation but a lot of it I have to go out and find for myself, through contact with tour companies, large businesses and the bigger hotels. Quite a lot of Blue Badge tour guides have their own websites but I haven't.

The training took two years, part-time, and it included lectures, practical sessions and visits and hours and hours of research and study at home. It takes a lot of dedication to get through the course, not to mention money [tuition fees are currently about £3,500]. There is so much to learn and remember – you wouldn't believe how much we're expected to know. But I was amazed to find that my mind sort of expanded to take it all in. It was remarkable.

I take people wherever they want to go in London and sometimes further afield, too. I have to be prepared to lead a tour anywhere that's reachable from London, so that includes day trips to places like Canterbury, Salisbury, Bath, Stonehenge, Oxford and Windsor.

Fortunately I really enjoy meeting people and helping them. One of the most important lessons I learned was that you can have all the knowledge in the world but if you can't put it across in a friendly, accessible way then you shouldn't be a guide. It's all about delivery.

How did it come about?

When my husband died I had to sell his car. I got talking to the woman who bought it and learnt she was a Blue Badge guide. She really inspired me, so I picked her brains about the training and took a guided tour of the British Museum so I could see a Blue Badge guide in action. It appealed to me so I registered with the Institute of Tourist Guiding [020 7953 1257 **www.itg.org.uk**] to start training as soon as possible.

Is it working out well for you?

Even better than I could have hoped. It's a job that I really would like to have started doing years ago because it ticks so many of my boxes. The nice thing is that I can tailor it to suit me – I can reduce the commitments, or even stop them for a while, if I want to see more of the family, and at other times I can step up the work and really be quite busy. There certainly isn't time to get bored because when I'm not working I'm reading up about places and piling more knowledge into my memory banks.

And the money?

It depends on what's being asked of me and how far afield I have to go, but on average I might clear about £200 a day, without tips.

PROS:

• Meeting such a wide variety of people from all over the world

• Learning and knowing so much about London

• Being in a position where I can help people and make a difference to their experience of visiting Britain

• I think it's made me a much more interesting person

• Discovering that I can pass exams in my 60s

• Having a job that keeps me fit and active and, above all, busy

CONS:

• Occasionally having to deal with difficult people

• The clothes. I really don't like having to dress to be practical and sensible – I prefer to be fashionable, but you can't totter about London in killer heels

• The fumes. I spend a lot of time shepherding people onto coaches while the engines are running and the exhaust fumes can be dreadful

- The rain. You really can't help getting soaked at Stonehenge when the rain is sweeping across Salisbury Plain. It can be very bleak at some times of the year

The TEFL teacher

Barbara, 71, formerly a freelance continuity girl for filmed commercials

Why are you still working?

I want to keep active and maintain contact with modern life. I live alone and would probably vegetate quickly without the discipline of a job. The money earned is also a motivation as it enables me to maintain a higher standard of living than would otherwise be possible.

What are you doing?

I work at a language school teaching English as a foreign language to overseas students, aged from late teens upwards. It is seasonal work, so that in summer I am very busy and for the first three months of the year it is very quiet indeed so I am not usually employed by the school through that period. For the rest of the year, April-December, I work mornings only from Monday to Friday, which amounts to about 15 hours of contact work per week plus all the preparation.

When I first started I worked full-time but this was not what I wanted long term. Unfortunately I had quite a battle to persuade the school to let me take afternoons off and had to officially leave before rejoining the staff some time later on a part-time basis. It suits me well now and I appreciate being able to have work breaks periodically.

The flow of work can be spasmodic as it depends on student numbers; if there is an international crisis, the school and teachers suffer accordingly. There is no pay if I am not actually working.

How did it come about?

I knew what I wanted to do post-retirement so it was all planned. I went to university to study English with Religious Studies because I wanted to top up my qualifications and had long wished to study at a higher level.

Twenty years earlier I had undergone TEFL training so now I retrained in readiness for my new career. One needs at least the Certificate in TEFL and a degree, preferably in English. The Certificate course is usually a very intensive four weeks, or some adult education centres offer a part-time version over one or two years. I did the four-week one.

In summer it is generally very easy to find jobs in language schools, especially along the south coast. The usual way of finding work is to send your CV to all language schools in the area and look in the *The Guardian* and the *Times Educational Supplement*.

Although these are usually temporary contracts they can become permanent if you fit in. When I went for interview I flatly refused to tell them my age. Fortunately, they were so desperate they took me anyway. Some months later they found out my age, I think through National Insurance details, but everyone seems happy and I'm still working!

Is it working out well for you?

Yes, it really is. If the students have enough English it is very interesting to talk to them about their views on life. Sometimes they are very knowledgeable about particular subjects and I can learn a lot from them. Ninety-nine percent of them are delightful.

I do a certain amount of preparation outside class and this could be at home or at the school. I really enjoy the lively atmosphere of the school.

And the money?

It's a lot less than I used to earn in the film industry but it pays for extras that I would otherwise not be able to afford.

The hourly rate is about £14.50. Some schools pay more, some less. If I had the next qualification up, the Diploma, I would earn a little more, but this would take me about two years to achieve, cost quite a lot and obviously would not be worth it in my case.

Because my income is so variable it makes sense to use an accountant.

PROS:

- Keeping in touch with the working world
- Being able to afford little extras
- Working with language keeps my brain active in that area
- Teaching classes keeps my speaking faculties up to scratch

CONS:

- Having to get up early every day
- Sometimes working outside of class is a bit irksome if I have other things I want to do

The clergyman

Michael, 67, on career no.5

Why are you still working?

I want to enjoy a worthwhile and rewarding retirement and continuing to work, albeit in a new career, is a very good way of achieving this.

What are you doing?

I am about to be ordained into the Ministry of the Church of England.

How did it come about?

I am following a calling.

Is it working out well for you?

As an ordained priest I anticipate with joy the wonderful freedom that my calling has brought me after living for so long under a shadow: I was invalided out of the Royal Navy at 32 and told I would not live beyond the age of 40. Tragedy struck later when my two stepchildren were killed in a road accident.

I was drawn to the Church but was still unsettled. After leaving submarines I became a stockbroker in the City, then joined a merchant bank but quit at 55 when the distaste for money-making became too strong. In due course I became the Royal British Legion welfare and fund-raising manager for the south-west of England.

For career no.5 I have undertaken a fairly rigorous training at theological college over three years and I am also taking a BA (Hons) degree in theology. It has been hard work, but very rewarding.

I live in a rural community once dominated by agriculture and I can see how far reaching the impact has been of the collapse of the farming industry. My hope is that, through the ministry, these people, many of them of middle age and in straitened circumstances, will be among those I can help. Their sense of loss of hope and trust in the future makes them feel they are in a sort of wilderness and I would like to play a role in restoring their confidence.

I will be working full-time, with two days off each week in lieu of Sundays. My wife will inevitably become involved in parish work, but she is very tolerant.

And the money?

I will be unpaid (non-stipendiary) at first but will in due course have the option to change to stipendiary status. The stipend varies a little from diocese to diocese but I would probably be looking at about £21,000 a year.

PROS:

- The satisfaction of answering a calling
- Fulfilling my 'retirement' ambition

CONS:

- I cannot see any at the moment

The customer service adviser

Vera 63, formerly a specialist programmer and data capture manager with a large plc

Why are you still working?

First and foremost I work because I don't feel as if I am ready yet for retirement. I keep very active and fortunately I'm in good health. My husband works abroad for a freight airline so he spends a lot of time away. I tell everyone I am still working because I don't want to become a full-time grandmother as I don't think I am ready for that yet. There are seven grandchildren who keep me busy when I'm not at work, so they could take over my life if I wasn't working.

What are you doing?

I work part-time for the general servicing team within Nationwide Life, a subsidiary of Nationwide Building Society. I deal with customer problems and corrections and do some telephone work. I find it very interesting as I'm dealing with customers and I get such a buzz out of sorting out their problems.

How did it come about?

It all started when I was 59 and approaching retirement. I got made redundant on a Friday and without a moment's hesitation I went straight to an employment agency (specialists in field staff). They actually wanted me to work for them but I didn't want to be high profile any more.

I was offered a position at Nationwide and started the following Monday. My husband was cross with me and said I could at least have taken a couple of weeks off, but he was away and I told him I would only work until he came home as we were going on holiday to Rhodes in three weeks' time.

After my holiday I returned to Nationwide as a temp but then they offered me a permanent position which I accepted because I liked the people and the environment. I was also very conscious that at Nationwide age is no barrier if you want to get on.

Is it working out well for you?

It's going really very well for me. I find the work very interesting and challenging and couldn't imagine anything would suit me better.

And the money?

I earn around £950 per month. It's really helpful to me because I've been a very keen line dancer for about 12 years and I go away a lot for weekends which could get expensive if I wasn't earning. I also play bingo and skittles a couple of times a week, so part of my salary goes towards that, too.

I'm quite good at shuffling my investments myself so I'm pretty comfortable with the financial side of things.

PROS:

• The working hours are very convenient and entirely flexible if, for instance, I have appointments that need to be kept

- Working with youngsters keeps me up to date with things in the big wide world – fashion, pop and things like that – so I'm in no danger of getting old before my time

- It's also quite nice if they have personal problems because being that bit older they ask my advice. It's good to feel wanted

CONS:

- Can't think of any

Nationwide Building Society was one of the first organisations to introduce flexible retirement. In 2001 it started to allow its older employees to work until 70, but since 2005 it extended this to 75. Those who choose to carry on working are entitled to their existing benefits.

The Society and its staff union both say they are "committed to diversity and recognise the valuable contribution older employees make to the business".

A Nationwide spokesman says research has shown that there is a strong correlation between employee satisfaction, customer satisfaction and the success of a business. "We have found that older employees help increase the levels of satisfaction amongst our customers. We also know that some employees wish to continue working beyond the normal retirement age, so have enhanced our policies to support those employees, giving them more choice over when they want to retire."

The Society has calculated that every 1% reduction in employee turnover represents an annual saving of £3 million.

Nationwide reports that 12% of its employees are aged 50 or over and it has about 160 employees over the age of 60 – a number that is increasing each year.

The life coach

Rosie, 60, formerly a vice principal of a sixth-form college

Why are you still working?

I had promised myself I would retire at 60 rather than go on to 65, however much I found myself enjoying the role when that point came. My reasons were that at that age I might still have the energy and drive to move into something different.

Until I came to retire I didn't know what that might be. The attraction of finding different challenges before finally donning the slippers was strong. This was partly because I'd always stayed in one career route and I didn't know if I could do anything else. I knew I'd have some fun finding out. I also fancied the more risky nature of this route, having never been a risk taker, but doing it with the safety net of a pension already in place.

I also knew I would greatly miss the contact with colleagues and students and felt I needed to substitute this with something more than just a little voluntary work, which although admirable I'm sure, would not have put me into the challenge zone enough to keep me thinking, planning and moving forward.

I was also attracted to the concept of greater freedom with my time. The opportunity to take off for Florence on a cheap air ticket when the fancy took me was also very strong. I hoped that at 60 all these things were possible, but maybe at 65 … who knows?

What are you doing?

I am soon to complete my DipNMC, a life and executive practitioner coach diploma. This has been by a combination of distance learning, residential and actual coaching practice. The course is designed to be completed in six to 18 months from start date, but I really want to power on and complete within eight months at the outside.

I am also, alongside this, developing some coaching work for the college and organisations who knew me when I was vice principal.

I have found it relatively easy to land not only some paid coaching work for senior managers in colleges who are newly in post but from that have designed a training course in coaching skills for senior managers which I am delivering to a local organisation.

At the moment, I have work for about two days a week but with the option of doing as much as I would like. I feel at present that this is ideal as it leaves some room for taking it easy and planning all those trips.

How did it come about?

With hindsight I had not given sufficient thought to what I should do but I did have the idea of asking my boss if he would go ahead with my annual appraisal a few months before my retirement even though it would be my last. He probably would have left it otherwise.

I requested that the main focus for this appraisal should be exploring with him what I might move into, and more specifically, and cheekily, how the college might be placed to help me achieve this.

The idea of life coaching came from the appraisal. My boss suggested it after telling me that I had been the best coach he had ever had on his staff and that he would have to think about consulting an external life coach when I left to fill this skills gap. This told me so much more than just giving me the initial idea: I realised my value in the coaching role, something I'd taken for granted as one of the main tasks of any senior manager, and also that he was happy to spend money to replace this skill in his college.

I wished then that I'd considered all this earlier but I put in some intensive research and found the course I'm on now.

I asked him if I could come back three months later to discuss my progress and see what I could offer the college. Being as up front as this takes a little courage but you have to do it.

I'm now close to qualifying and the college has already given me paid coaching work. In addition I approached another organisation (where my old boss is on the Board and would vouch for the quality of my contribution) to ask if I could deliver the 50 hours of coaching to their staff which I needed as part of my course. They were glad to take the free coaching and on the strength of feedback from it they then asked me to deliver a training course to their senior managers on coaching skills in the work place.

I now feel I can move on to approaching other local colleges, especially while they still know me from my vice principal role and I have a good reputation.

The point here is that if you have a reputation in your area then you need to use it – and very quickly, as everything is transient and, sadly, you are soon forgotten in the old networks.

I intend to build a new, equally strong, reputation for coaching in the corporate arena as well as investigating work for private clients and work in other venues such as gyms and fitness centres.

Is it working out well for you?

So far, absolutely. I'm doing something which in truth I know I can do well, and I haven't let time go by too quickly before cashing in on previous reputation – sort of rippling out from what was a strong centre ground for me.

The cost has been considerable, about £3,000 with fees and other costs, but I've already made 60% of that back and am sure I can reclaim the rest very quickly. In addition I've greatly enjoyed the learning, and meeting a range of people also on the course, some of whom are email buddies now and we help each other where we can.

It is very important, in my view, to enrol on to a good course as there are so many of them out there. It is also important to register with the European Coaching Institute, which gives much practical advice, and to get professional indemnity insurance for when dealing with clients, especially if coaching under-18s.

The most valuable thing that has come from what I'm doing is the surge in confidence I've experienced from going through the life coaching course. I've really felt the sense of what I might do in my career, but also my life, in the future. I've had some valuable insights which have changed me for ever.

And the money?

Difficult to be too precise as I haven't built my website yet or really promoted my business, but 10 hours a week at £40 per hour will be bringing me in about £20,000 a year. I've always done my own tax return but will probably get an accountant for the first year or so in the hope I can pick up some useful tips from which I could learn enough to do my own tax return later if I wanted.

PROS:

- The work is related to my previously strong areas
- The course is flexible and can be done when I want
- I'm learning so much about myself that I am increasing my own levels of self-worth and confidence (pity my poor long-suffering partner!)
- I love working with people and can develop a rapport easily with them so I know I can do this work
- I take real pleasure from seeing clients move forward – and that has happened already

- My brain has a new challenge and I therefore feel energised
- I'm not thinking or talking much about my old job – a real plus if you want to avoid appearing really sad
- All my coaching appointments can be arranged to suit me

CONS:

- Only having to pay the course fee of £2,350, but it was worth it – and I've nearly earned it all back already

The resident landlady

Yvonne, 70, formerly a practice nurse in a GP's surgery

Why are you still working?

For something to do and for the money.

What are you doing?

I let out two rooms in my house. The tenants share a bathroom and my rooms are all on the ground floor so we don't run into each other more than we want to. Both the tenants are men – one's in his 30s, a post-graduate student at the university, and the other is in his late 20s and is training to do something with the theatre.

I supply them with clean bed linen and towels once a week and sometimes if either of them is here on a Sunday I'll pop in and ask them down for a bite of lunch with me. I like that and I think they appreciate it, too. I don't charge them for that, obviously, but they usually bring a bottle of wine or something, and that's nice.

How did it come about?

I have a couple of friends who do this so I thought I'd follow their example. It seemed a sensible thing to do with the spare rooms. I'm widowed and the family all live close enough not to need to come and stay here, so I don't feel guilty about denying them the opportunity.

Is it working out well for you?

Yes. I've been doing it for seven years now and I'm up to tenant number five, so there isn't a great turnover. They all seem to be very nice and we respect each other's space. There haven't been any wild parties – yet!

And the money?

It's all taxable, of course, but I keep very careful records and I do my own tax return. I clear about £7,500 a year, which isn't a huge amount but it certainly makes it worthwhile. Quite a lot of things are tax deductible, such as repairs, wear and tear and replacing towels and the like.

PROS:

- It has added a new dimension to my life
- The money, which is very useful
- Keeping my brain active when I do the books and complete my tax return
- Interesting conversations with the tenants
- Sometimes it's just nice to know there's someone else in the house

CONS:

- Quite a lot of initial outlay on preparing the rooms for tenants
- Taking a chance on the suitability of tenants
- Having to keep the books constantly up to date
- Being responsible for meeting health and safety and fire regulations

Letting a room in your home as a means of getting extra income is worth considering because it is fairly straightforward – once you've established your position regarding the various obligations to a tenant and, of course, the terms and conditions of your mortgage lender and insurer. If your home is rented from a council or housing association you would need to obtain permission to let a room.

You will need to be aware that The Disability Discrimination Act, Sex Discrimination Act and Race Relations Act apply to a resident landlord and that you are responsible for repairs to such things as wash basins and lavatories. Fire hazards won't be tolerated and a landlord must also ensure that gas and electrical appliances are completely safe.

Anyone renting out a furnished room in their home may take advantage of the optional exemption scheme called Rent a Room, which allows a landlord a certain amount of tax free gross income (currently £4,250). However, if you opt to join this scheme you cannot then claim the cost of household repairs or insurance, for example, against tax. You would need to weigh up whether opting in or out of Rent a Room would work best for you. Take advice from a letting agent and try and talk with other landlords and see which option they have gone for. Find out more on **www.direct.gov.uk** and put 'Rent a Room' into the search facility.

The sales adviser and coach

Valerie, 66, formerly an assistant bank manager

Why are you still working?

Three reasons:

1 There have been a number of changes in taxation that have affected my finances

2 I have remarried

3 My husband and I have a mortgage to service

What are you doing?

I'm a sales adviser and coach with Marks & Spencer, working on general merchandise. I cover the till, customer services and fitting rooms. I work a minimum of 29 hours a week plus additional hours if required.

How did it come about?

At the age of 60, I found that because of tax changes I needed to work to pay our mortgage. The only company out of those I wrote to seeking work who offered me an interview was M&S. The interview made me aware that age was not a barrier. I was offered temporary employment as Christmas staff and was given a permanent contract in the January. Marks & Spencer were five years ahead of other companies in their attitude towards older employees.

Is it working out well for you?

Very well indeed. It is very much a team store and I am happy to be the deputy chairman of my store's Business Involvement Group. [M&S's BIGs are employee representation forums at local, divisional and national level, from where some go on to sit on the European Works Council. One of the many policy changes brought about as a result of feedback from the forums is the payment of staff for good performance rather than their length of service.]

And the money?

I get paid £6.40 per hour. For my basic 29-hour week, without overtime or anything, that works out at £185.60 per week .

I complete an annual tax return to cover my bank pension, state pension and my income from Marks & Spencer.

PROS:

- The money is really useful. It enables us to have holidays and not feel guilty and it gives me the chance to save, too

CONS:

- I have absolutely nothing against what I do and where I work, but I would like to get back into office work

The classroom assistant

Peter, 60, formerly a Commander in the Royal Navy

Why are you still working?

Three reasons:

1 To regain some self-respect and identity; after leaving a career in which responsibility, leadership and management were key features it felt very strange to wake up and have nothing worthwhile to do.

2 Having settled back again into living in Plymouth, I felt that I wanted to put something back into the community.

3 A little pocket money for the treats in life.

What are you doing?

My priority on leaving the Royal Navy at the age of 53 (the compulsory leaving age has since risen to 55) was to take some time out, get to know my family again (we had spent nearly half of my career living apart from one another) especially as my last job had entailed five years of living in Southampton and working seven-day weeks for six weeks at a time. I was also anxious to finish a lay preacher's course I had started at Southampton. I was finally licensed a week before moving house.

I sought several jobs in the university sector and, whilst always getting to the final interview stage, never got a final offer of a job. Behind the scenes checks made on my behalf by friends indicated that I was 'too experienced – he'll be after my job' or too old and male 'we're a young all-girl team' – a team that looked after one faculty's entire undergraduate admissions. There were also comments that I was taking easy jobs – which was correct, I had worked myself to the bone in the Service and had no wish to repeat that.

Thanks to my 28 years in the Navy, in a career that spanned training, personnel and budgetary management, engineering and diving during various appointments at sea, training establishments and at the Ministry of Defence in London, I had plenty of qualifications and experience. I was also IT literate to a high level but was failed on two occasions by the lack of a modern computer qualification – the fact that I had taught it at Southampton had no relevance.

By chance I found myself applying for a teaching assistant post at a local primary school – the post essentially involved teaching various software tools to the youngsters and looking after the school's computer network system. I have been working there for the past two years and am thoroughly enjoying myself.

I work three days a week except when I am helping to run week-long courses on Dartmoor or residential courses which inevitably turn out to be an 80-hour week.

I have had a steep learning curve insofar as the children are concerned (it is an inner city school with an above average percentage of single parent families and non-English speaking parents) and the computer networking side, but I seem to manage.

Despite the grey beard, I am fully accepted by all the staff and the presence of a man in the school is, apparently, having a good effect. I certainly seem to see more than a fair share of first aid customers and get a lot of knee hugs (I am over six feet tall and most kids are not much more than three feet) – the politically correct routine of 'no touching' is taught to the staff but ignored at appropriate moments in public. Despite the low level of academics (by post-graduate engineering standards), I feel fulfilled and have re-established my identity.

How did it come about?

I saw the job advertised in my local paper and just thought I'd give it a try.

Is it working out well for you?

Yes, I think it is. I originally started at three and a half days a week but have negotiated the same hours over three consecutive days – giving me a longer weekend. I have requested leave during term time (four weeks in Canada for a holiday and two single weeks for Christian Mission work) and have always had it granted.

As a lay preacher in a local church I am often involved in various classroom activities dealing with Christianity – stories, explanations and customs – and regularly host visits by the school to my church.

Having long weekends means quality time with my wife in our caravan in Cornwall; the chance to visit people for a decent length of time and to be at home for my two grandchildren. I hope to be a better grandad than I was a dad.

And the money?

After tax, I am earning around £440 a month which, with my RN pension, allows us those little extras. Considering the scope of the work, it really is peanuts and most teaching assistants deserve far more.

PROS:

- Restored self-esteem with a chance to put something back into the community

- A chance to make a difference to some poorly resourced and needy children
- An opportunity to keep my brain active
- Opportunities for good quality time with my family and my local church

CONS:

- Poor financial reward for the level of technical support I give to the school
- The working environment (dusty and dry and the children) gives rise to a hacking cough and heavy cold every November, often involving a week's lay off – first in my life

The councillor

Sue, 71, formerly a deputy headteacher

Why are you still working?

I wanted to keep active, play a part in the community and do something useful.

What are you doing?

I'm a councillor, an elected member of the borough council for the large conurbation where I live. I've been appointed the borough's Older People's Champion and I'm on two of the council's scrutiny panels (Education and Lifelong Learning and Developing Communities and Tackling Crime).

How did it come about?

I've always been a busy sort of person. I trained first as a nurse and then as a teacher and retired at 55 as deputy head of a middle school where I taught science and coached and umpired netball to national level. I'd also served on the Sports Council and been county president of the National Union of Teachers.

Early retirement gave me more time to spend with my husband and our two sons and their families as well as to pursue some of my many interests, such as skiing, sailing, aerobics, playing table tennis and running with the Hash House Harriers. I always aim to try something new every year, so at the moment I'm learning to play bridge.

After my husband died I began to feel I'd like to put something back into the community. I thought this would probably take the form of helping serve the coffee and tidy away the chairs at my local community centre. But someone else thought differently and decided to make use of my energy by encouraging me to stand for the council. No one was more surprised than me when I was elected.

Is it working out well for you?

It's busy, but it suits me. I love it. I'm on almost permanent call for everyone in the large, very mixed residential area that I represent and I spend many hours every week calling on people in their homes to hear their grievances and take up their cases or just to have a friendly chat. I could drown in the gallons of tea I get through in a week.

The learning curve has been astonishingly steep. I've had to become knowledgeable about so many areas of life – things like transport and health, planning issues and all the latest legislation. Fortunately, I learned to speed read at university so that helps me when I'm faced with 50-page briefing documents and big, thick reports that I need to read before meetings.

As a number of my fellow councillors are in full-time employment and, in some cases, have family commitments, too, I can see how fortunate I am. It is a tremendous advantage being retired.

A vital tool in my armoury for coping with all my activities is a daily To Do list. I spend about 15 minutes compiling this each morning and then work through it methodically until bedtime. Anything left undone is added to the list for the following day. I learnt the importance of a To Do list when I was a deputy head, because when you're managing people you have to have a clear idea of everything that needs to be achieved.

Another aid I use is a timer: I allow myself one hour on the computer and, once the timer has buzzed, I turn off my PC. It's not good to be sedentary for any longer and so I make sure I get all my emails read and written in that time. I also make swift phone calls and use mobile phone texting as a time-efficient means of communication.

I really relish the chance to improve the lives of so many of the older residents. I talk to them wherever I go: the library, the sports centre, the launderette. The launderette is *the* place for a good natter, believe me. Basically, their overwhelming need is to be made to feel safe, and that's the challenge I've taken up on their behalf.

As for making money from being a councillor, I can safely say I'm never going to be rich as a result of all the work. While the allowance may make a difference to my annual income, the hours of hard work and commitment mean that I'm on an hourly rate that would probably equate with what small boys earned when they were sent up chimneys. But I'm not complaining. I don't have time for that.

And the money?

After my election, the next surprise came when I discovered I was entitled to an allowance of £7,500 a year. I had absolutely no idea there was such a thing. I really didn't know I'd get any money other than my travel expenses, so it was a very pleasant discovery to make.

And I'd be lying if I said it didn't make a difference, because it does. I have only a modest pension so, at my stage of life, this extra sum is very welcome.

PROS:

- Meeting people
- Broadening the mind
- Educational
- Fulfilling
- Close involvement with the community
- Having a voice
- Being able to influence things for the good of the town
- Putting into practice so many of the life skills acquired over the years
- Exercising pensioner power
- The financial benefits
- Having the opportunity to make a difference
- Feeling needed

CONS:

- Very time consuming
- Time and space are too often not one's own
- Frustrating that party politics play too large a part in local government
- Overwhelming amounts of paperwork
- Not enough hours in the day

The B&B owners

Louis, 67, formerly a self-employed electrician, and Jenny, also 67, formerly a care assistant in a residential home for the elderly

Why are you still working?

We always knew we would do something to keep us busy in retirement, for our health's sake and for an income, which we badly need. I couldn't afford to keep myself up to date with all the new rules and regulations for electricians, otherwise I might have worked on for longer.

What are you doing?

We run a Bed & Breakfast in our home in a seaside village. There are three bedrooms, one with an en suite bathroom, and the other two rooms share a bathroom. They are all on the first floor and we have our own bedroom and bathroom on the top floor. Downstairs we've a lounge, dining room, kitchen and a sun room at the back, looking over the garden. It's a beautiful house, built in the early 1800s and very pretty. We've lived here since we were married and this is where we brought up our two sons and a daughter, who've obviously all moved out now but we're lucky as they don't live far away. Our daughter's only in the next village.

We have guests mainly from Easter through to the October half-term, with only a handful in total during the rest of the year. Lots of them are people who've been coming to us for their annual break since we opened seven years ago and they've become good friends. Others find us through calling in at the Tourist Information office or else via our own website, which our daughter is in charge of, or through any of the council or tourist association accommodation guides. We're in plenty of those. Then there's word of mouth. People might call in at a pub and ask for a recommendation for a

B&B and come to us that way, or maybe they've had friends who have stayed with us.

It's hard work, running a B&B, and it certainly isn't an easy way to make money. But we're happy with it as it suits us well and it has meant we haven't had to move out of our home which, had we bought a smaller place, would have been the only other option for us to realise some money for our old age.

We spent £4,500 on doing up the house – redecorating, updating the bathrooms, installing wall mounted TVs, that sort of thing – before we opened, and it was money well spent. People like a nice bathroom with a really good shower probably as much as they like a well furnished bedroom. And we invested in good quality sheets and towels, too, as they can really let a place down if they're cheap and shabby.

We took some tips from places we'd stayed in and liked, and used some of their ideas. We thought it was a good investment to travel around a bit and pick up little nuggets, sometimes from asking but usually just from observing. For instance, a rug on the hall floor doesn't only enhance the décor but it can help prevent wet or muddy footprints going upstairs. And we've no dried flowers any-where (they're so depressing!) – just fresh ones, mostly from the garden.

We're probably pitched just below the middle of the market, no higher because we don't have any car parking space and there are no sea views.

Our day starts at 5.30am when I go and get the papers and fresh eggs for our guests' breakfast. Jenny always offers a cooked break-fast with home-made bread, her own jam and marmalade as well as cereals and fruit.

Clearing up breakfast and doing the rooms takes up most of the morning, with both of us involved. We like everything to be absolutely spotless. A lot of our time is spent changing the beds and dealing with the laundry. We may have a little time to ourselves after lunch, if there aren't any DIY or extra cleaning jobs or shopping that needs doing, and then it's time to start preparing the evening meal. We like to offer dinner as well, as long as the guests book at breakfast time. It's another way to earn some pennies, but we'll probably stop doing it next year. It's a lot of extra work.

After dinner, which Jenny and I both prepare and serve, we grab a bite to eat and then clear up, usually finishing around 11pm.

Luckily neither of us seems to need a great deal of sleep, which is just as well.

We enjoy meeting new people all the time and there are few downsides, only a TV remote control going home in someone's luggage and a couple who broke the no smoking rule, thinking no one would mind if they smoked while leaning out of their bedroom window. We did mind!

Our hours of work are a bit mad considering what we earn from it, but we've nothing much else to do with our time so we might as well be doing this, which we like. It's a lot quieter in the winter, and that's when we give ourselves a break and go down to Spain to spend a month in a hotel and have someone wait on us for a change.

How did it come about?

Our daughter Jackie suggested it. She shared our concern about not wanting to move and she did a lot of work for us, finding out what was required in the way of health and safety, fire regulations and the like, how to publicise the B&B and that sort of thing. She organised the website too, and keeps it all up to date for us. We're glad she does all that as we don't have a computer ourselves.

We are fortunate that we're in such a good location. There are plenty of popular attractions close by so there's always a need for B&Bs in an area like ours.

Is it working out well for you?

Yes. We get on well working together and we have strengths in different areas. For instance, Jenny's great at breakfasts, I'm not bad at dinners, and we're both good at making the guests feel welcome and comfortable. I think the only thing that would make it better would be if we could afford to pay someone to deal with all the laundry. It's never ending.

And the money?

It makes a lot of difference – not that we have much time during the peak periods to spend any of it! If we're full seven nights running, including the child's put-u-up in the larger room, we can take £840. That's the maximum and we'd only expect that during August. The rest of the summer we average about £500 a week.

There are a lot of costs to come out of that but they can mostly be offset against tax. I use the same accountant as when I was self-employed and for the professionalism and peace of mind it's money well spent.

PROS:

- We haven't had to move from our family home
- We're doing something that plays to our strengths
- The money is very welcome for our future security
- We're never likely to be lonely
- Meeting so many good people

CONS:

- Being tired throughout the summer
- Our time and our home are never our own

Chapter 6

Variation on a theme

This is the option where you go for a little more of the same. Whatever work you choose to do post-retirement is related to what you used to do, albeit at a different speed. You may be continuing in the same general direction but you change lanes – and adapt to survive.

On the face of it, it should be the easiest way not just to find work but actually to do the work. It should be well within your capabilities, for a start. You would have few doubts that you could do work that you've mostly been doing before anyway, and it is possible that you would keep some of your old colleagues, contacts and friends if your new job overlaps in any way with the old.

The advantages are considerable. All those years of building up knowledge, making it second nature, capitalising on your instinct and being at ease in your work will stand you in good stead.

Opting for work that is on a familiar theme may seem less challenging but it makes a lot of sense. But as you tweak your personal sat-nav to take you cruising from the fast lane to at least the middle lane, you may like to consider beefing up your life by bolting on a new dimension, perhaps through some voluntary work or by starting a new hobby. Not experiencing the stimulating thrill of stepping into the unknown, such as would come with taking a new direction, you might feel inclined to compensate by stretching yourself in other ways.

Simon [see his case study below] went into consultancy work in a field closely associated with his career but has taken up rollerblading, too, and has learnt to play the electric guitar. He also handles the PR for a young motor racing driver with Formula One ambitions, and that's on top of the sailing and travelling that he has always enjoyed. A full and busy retirement indeed.

The career transition consultant

Simon, 59, formerly head of human resources for a blue chip financial services company

Why are you still working?

A combination of circumstances. I thought I really had retired one Christmas and had no intention of working again. The next year was a glorious year which I spent like a child on school holidays – doing things that I never had time for when I was in corporate life.

Soon, however, a number of things happened. Firstly, I realised I was missing some of the daily human contact of business life. (Finding you're listening for the postman so you can go out for a chat is a bit of a clue to that.) Secondly, I was having to plan carefully to fund some aspects of the lifestyle I enjoyed when I was working. And thirdly, I found that while I was saying to people 'I'm retired', my wife, who was still working, was saying things like 'He's on a sabbatical' or 'He's having a gap year'.

As a result of this I started to think very tentatively about doing something – and then I had an approach [see below].

What are you doing?

I work for a consultancy that provides a service to companies that are making people redundant – it used to be called 'outplacement' but now goes under the flashier name of 'career transition'. I work with people who have been made redundant, helping them come to terms with what has happened, identify their strengths, decide what they want to do and then make sure they achieve it.

It often involves coaching them in the skills required to get another job (developing their CV, how to approach the job market, preparing for interview, etc) or it might involve setting up a business (challenging their idea, developing a business plan, marketing, accounts, tax etc).

Some clients just want to retire and I help them understand the implications of this and prepare for it. Others head for what we call a 'portfolio lifestyle' – perhaps a couple of days a week in paid employment, a small business needing a few hours a month, a bit of voluntary work and a lot of lovely leisure time. This is becoming increasingly popular for people once they reach the age of 50.

I spend one to two days a week in face-to-face meetings with clients and perhaps half a day or more at home doing admin, updating systems and arranging appointments.

How did it come about?

I had a call from a company that knew of me and knew I'd retired. They said they wanted someone with "a few grey hairs", so that was encouraging. They took me on initially to handle their top end (directors, chief executives etc) which would have meant about a couple of days a month. I found I enjoyed the work so much, however, that I now take on clients at all levels and consequently am doing more days than initially anticipated.

Is it working out well for you?

Yes – very. I get great satisfaction from what I do. It's interesting and challenging but carries none of the stresses of corporate life. I really look forward to my working day and enjoy a quality of work/life balance that I've never had before.

And the money?

It makes some difference but is not used for anything that could be regarded as normal or routine expenditure. I am conscious that the work could come to an end at any time (be that my decision or theirs) and I was determined to ensure that I did not start to rely on the income from it in any way.

My mind has been very clear on this from the outset so the money is kept completely separate from other funds and is spent only on specific things that could be regarded as pure luxuries or one-offs – 'treats' if you like.

I went to see an accountant when I was setting up as self-employed. He was refreshingly honest and told me that I didn't need him. He suggested that I simply set up a few spreadsheets for my accounts and I have developed these gradually so that they now provide me with the precise figures I need for my tax return.

PROS:

- Provides an additional intellectual challenge and interest in my life
- Gives me immense satisfaction
- Puts me in front of interesting people with interesting problems
- Provides money for things I would otherwise not be able to afford
- Hopefully makes me less daunting to sit next to at parties ('So, what do you do?' 'I'm retired' can be something of a conversation stopper …)

CONS:

- The admin work, for which I cannot charge, becomes a bit of a drag

- Doing some of the work at home means that it can gradually impose on your personal life without your realising it

- I sometimes over-deliver, meaning that I do more for a client than I am able to charge for – I have to remember that I am not a charity

- Although I am working only part-time, I seem to be busier than at any other stage in my life. I think, though, that that's more to do with having an enjoyable retirement than the particular job I'm doing

The social worker

Patsy, 64, formerly a social worker in a different county

Why are you still working?

For two reasons: we need the money (see below) and I am scared to stop working. My fear comes from the fact that my mother retired and then died two years later.

What are you doing?

I am a social worker in a busy children and families team. I work from 8.45am until 5.15pm every weekday. It is quite a punishing routine at my age, and I quite often look after my grandchildren at weekends, too. I also have to be 'on duty' to supervise my husband in the garden and when carrying out home improvements, so I am extremely busy.

How did it come about?

I sought out a social services department that would take me on at a time when I would have been expected to retire, and we moved house so I could accept the appointment and carry on working.

Is it working out well for you?

Yes.

And the money?

I work very hard but I feel well rewarded for all the effort and for my years of experience. My income is necessary as my husband took early retirement 10 years ago and our mortgage isn't due to end until 2013.

PROS:

- We have good holidays
- I can help out the children financially
- I don't have to think before I buy – if I need something, I buy it

CONS:

- Everyone is dependent on me and I feel obliged to carry on for ever. This scares me

> Patsy's feeling of obligation to keep on working indefinitely could make her vulnerable to stress, or certainly suffer some stress related symptoms. She says she is scared by the expectation that falls upon her to carry on bringing home the wherewithal to keep a roof over their heads and to finance the children from time to time. Added to this is her fear of stopping work because her mother died only two years after retiring and she doesn't want the same fate to befall her.

> Many would empathise, and certainly sympathise. The fact that Patsy recognises the burden she bears is good, for trouble lies in store for anyone who cannot recognise why they feel trapped on a treadmill. Acknowledging the causes of being cornered and put upon is one thing. Handling the resentment and feelings of fear that result is quite another.

> Patsy is fortunate that she loves her job and is comfortable with it. She

works hard, she says, but it is all within her capabilities. When dealing with stress it is important to have coping mechanisms, and Patsy's job satisfaction is an obvious bonus in this respect. If she was unhappy at work, her situation would be many times worse and she'd be having to seek help and devise more strategies to enable her to cope.

The teacher

Sue, 62, formerly head of psychology at an independent school for girls

Why are you still working?

I am still active and enjoy working. If I have the genes of the women in my mother's family, I could live for another 30 years. I get very depressed if I am not able to keep active, and I am an extrovert so I like being surrounded by people, being part of a school community. I really am not ready for retirement. Apart from the intellectual stimulation, I want to keep earning. We have had three children who are now financially independent, but it was expensive seeing them through university. We have had a few years when we didn't have to worry about money and could afford good holidays.

I would like a few more years of earning a good salary before I have to manage on a pension, especially as my state pension is going to be £33 a week (because I opted to pay married women's stamp) and my teaching pension about £7,000 (because I took out my superannuation when we had three children under four and were very hard up).

What are you doing?

I was forced to leave my job at the end of the academic year in which I was 60. All teaching staff, men and women, had contracts which stipulated that they had to retire at 60. The Head said there was nothing personal in making me retire, but she was just applying the rules and could not set a precedent by letting me continue working.

Some of my colleagues were very happy to retire at 60 and thought I was mad to want to go on working. Also, there was some ageism from younger colleagues who thought 60 year olds were past it. My students, both past and present, have encouraged me to believe I am not past it. I have no doubt that I will keep active one way or another after I eventually do retire.

Now, I'm lucky to be employed as a psychology teacher in a state comprehensive school, on a 0.7 contract – ie I could not get a full-time job and so my salary has been reduced by a third, although the Head tried to match pro rata what I was earning

This job has entailed an enormous amount of work because the school was in Special Measures and had gone through a very difficult period with very disruptive pupils. The Head, brought in to turn things around, set up a sixth form but could not get a psychology teacher, so I am trying to make up for lost time with resits, introducing a new syllabus and also teaching four courses I have never taught before, three of them in a new subject to make up my hours.

I also work for World Challenge organising expeditions for a grammar school in another town, which involves a 60-mile round trip for every meeting.

How did it come about?

When I realised it was inevitable that I was going to lose my job (I had appealed to the governors, gone to the Citizens Advice Bureau, asked my union and phoned a solicitor), I sent my CV to all schools and colleges within a wide radius of home. I am fortunate that I was able to help myself. My new Head phoned almost immediately and offered me a job. He said he was delighted to employ someone with my wealth of experience. I was also offered a job at the grammar school mentioned above, but for fewer hours. It would have been much easier, but involved too much driving, so I turned it down. However, the Head there wanted to run World Challenge expeditions and didn't have a teacher who would organise them, so World Challenge asked me to act as a local area manager for them. I agreed because I hope to go on a future expedition (maybe Brazil). I can't run one in my current school because it is in a relatively deprived area and the students would probably not be able to raise the cost of taking part.

Is it working out well for you?

Yes – so far! The Head at my new school has done an amazing job of turning the school around. Nevertheless I am having to deal with younger students than I am used to, and behaviour that I would not have been faced with in my former job. I have had to work very hard indeed to plan lessons. I have told the Head that I will try to work there for another four years, but I may not be able to do so without affecting my pension. Teachers' pensions are calculated on the best year of their last three years of earning, and of course I'm earning less because I'm part-time so it wouldn't make financial sense for me to do more than two years.

The staff have been very welcoming and supportive and I think the job will be there for me as long as I want it, although the hours may decrease. I probably won't carry on with the World Challenge work for too long because there will be an age limit to sleeping in hammocks in the jungle and trekking with a full back pack!

And the money?

My take-home pay from the teaching job for one average month is £1,373.70. This is clearly a significant amount, more than many people get working full-time. I save £500 a month, and we are still paying off a mortgage. We also have good holidays.

World Challenge pays me £10 an hour, which probably amounts to around £500 a year (though I could get more work with them if I wanted it). I do it because I will be able to go on expeditions, which is worth about £3,000 every time I take part.

I have not taken either of my pensions yet and am still paying pension contributions.

PROS:

- Still feeling relatively young, active and involved
- Still able to save, pay for holidays, and buy nice Christmas presents
- I feel that I have financial independence and security
- I have been able to attend a painting course on my day off

CONS:

- I am working harder for less pay
- I am sometimes very tired
- I have withdrawn from some of my hobby activities because of the pressure

The educational consultant

Barry, 57, formerly headteacher of a pupil referral unit

Why are you still working?

Because I can't afford not to.

What are you doing?

I run my own educational consultancy/training business for schools in the UK, with the focus on training teaching assistants in special educational needs and behaviour.

How did it come about?

I was completely fed up with the local education authority (LEA) and levels of interference and apparent incompetence. I retired one year before the minimum age of retirement in teaching (which is 55), at which point I took an actuary reduced pension.

I tested the water first by running courses for the LEA then went out on my own. Now I use the skills and strengths I gained through all my years of work in the sphere of education.

Is it working out well for you?

Yes. I have a minimum amount of money I require to live on. I exceed that amount every month and so save my pension. Some weeks I work five days, some weeks only two days. And I only work during school terms.

And the money?

I earn more now than when I was a headteacher. The market is big so I could expand but I don't need to.

For about the past 10 years I have also been running a small buy-to-let business, which in time will supplement my actuary reduced pension both in capital and income terms.

When I was vice principal of a technology college I took a year out and worked for Britannic Assurance. This gave me a good insight into financial matters, but I still wouldn't be without an accountant.

PROS:

- Being my own boss
- Easy to maintain quality
- Making a difference
- Meet lots of new people

- Making good money
- Travelling to every town in the UK and staying in good hotels
- Playing golf

CONS:

- Travel can be tiring but I have a good car
- I have to be very well organised and disciplined
- Playing golf badly

The editorial assistant

Diana, 67, formerly a secretary

Why are you still working?

I need to be with people and have a purpose in my life. This is my lifeline – something stimulating to get up for in the morning and a great boon on those long, dreary winter days. After my husband died I really felt the loss of contact with the outside world. What I needed was the buzz of being in an office with colleagues. I am not the sort who goes to coffee mornings as a pastime.

What are you doing?

I'm working as a part-time (all day Tuesdays and Wednesdays) editorial assistant for a weekly newspaper group. I also get called in to cover sometimes if anyone is off sick or on holiday. My main job is to collate the what's on listings for three newspapers and prepare readers' letters for publication. There's a lot of word processing involved. I also do a great deal of phone answering and I process and answer many of the hundreds of emails that come into the office each week.

How did it come about?

I live only 100 metres from the office so I was always passing. One day I called in to offer my services. If you're a good copy typist, which I am, it's amazing how useful you can be. Also, I am easily contactable by phone so can come in at a few minutes' notice, I'm reliable and I don't need to be told how to do something more than once. I've taken computers and new technology in my stride and I think that's very important.

Is it working out well for you?

Overall, it's great. I enjoy the pace and nature of the work and the fact it keeps my brain active.

And the money?

I'm on a reasonable hourly rate – no complaints, but I haven't had a rise for years. It's time I plucked up the courage to ask if there's anything left in the pot for me. If you don't ask you don't get. What I earn pays for a lot of extras which means I don't have to dip into my capital. It is a definite bonus.

PROS:

- It's nice to feel wanted and useful
- To know I'm making a difference

CONS:

- Although I can only see good things about my job, I do sometimes slightly resent not having more freedom to take holidays, but if I wasn't working I couldn't afford them anyway

The fitness teacher

Elizabeth, 70, formerly a trainer, course director and City & Guilds examiner for remedial exercise therapists

Why are you still working?

Because I'm in demand. Also, everyone in my classes enjoys themselves and it enables me to keep myself fit in body and mind. I keep in touch with the outside world, too, and of course it's a useful source of income.

What are you doing?

I was originally a teacher of PE and dance in schools and now I take day and evening classes in Fitness League exercise and dance and in Pilates.

I was compulsorily retired by the county council education department at the age of 65 but I have continued to teach privately.

My teaching work amounts to nine hours a week, but of course there's the travel and preparation on top. Some weekends are spent away on residential refresher courses or five-day residential courses because the government requires all qualified teachers to undergo CPD – continuing professional development.

How did it come about?

Work for me has really been continuous since being at dancing school at the age of three. I did teacher training and continued to study and train in relevant subjects while working for various education departments.

I have helped work come to me by keeping my name to the fore through TV appearances and radio interviews and writing articles.

Is it working out well for you?

Very well. I am very fortunate.

And the money?

I net about £40–£60 a week, depending on the time of year. There are occasional extra amounts of between £30 and £80 earned through lectures. The money goes towards holidays and running a car and helps with the costs of a shared ownership holiday home. It makes quite a difference to us as my husband had to retire early after suffering a number of strokes.

PROS:

- No time to get bored or to have miserable days
- My work has kept my LSD – life space diameter – wide and interesting
- I have travelled to several countries as well as throughout the UK on group holidays and had lots of fun on the way, mixing with all ages from our various classes

CONS:

- Not much time for a break – perhaps four weeks a year, or five if I'm lucky
- Time spent on preparation of class work or notes for students
- Playing endless CDs and cassettes to help me select a variety of music to suit all ages

Chapter 7

A hobby extended

It is quite possible to base a money-making venture on your hobby. If you've been happily filling your spare time with, say, training dogs, framing pictures or threading beads to make beautiful necklaces for friends, you could certainly expand your activities and make them into money spinners.

There are many people who retire with a huge sigh of relief, rub their hands and crack on gratefully with the activity that has been their part-time passion for a number of years. Ridding themselves of the work routine means they can now get closer than ever before to the hobby that has absorbed them for all-too-brief sessions at weekends and occasional evenings, only when time has allowed.

Retirement brings the freedom they've been itching for. Whether it's a table-top production or something on a larger scale, hobby-based work is ideal as a part-time or even full-time venture because it evolves from two important elements: knowledge and passion.

Careful research is, of course, a vital component too, and it is as well to heed the warnings of those who have tried to develop their hobby only to find it stalled in the starting blocks. There was the couple who, having bred a beautiful litter of King Charles spaniel puppies from their pet, Holly, decided that a little occasional puppy breeding could significantly bolster their pensions and that two of Holly's offspring could hold the key to a regular little fortune if they kept them and in due course bred from them.

While mentally counting their shiny new pennies, they looked into what would be involved in setting up as breeders, albeit on a very small scale. They quickly stopped counting and cancelled the Ferrari. They discovered that to breed dogs on anything more than an occasional basis you need to be registered and hold a licence and costs escalate dramatically. The whole venture rapidly fizzled out and died and, perhaps appropriately for puppy owners, they started looking into buying a carpet cleaning franchise.

The fish breeder

Brian, 60, formerly an executive with a publishing group

Why are you still working?

For many reasons: first of all, I was only 56 when I retired, so I needed to do something constructive. My 'work' centres on the breeding of various unusual species of tropical fish, which has been my hobby for more than 30 years. So I have been doing this on a casual or hobby basis for a long time and would be stepping this up by choice now that I have more free time anyway. But I am also glad of a little extra income because my company pension is far less than my salary but my appetite for the good things in life, such as decent cars and holidays, remains undiminished.

What are you doing?

I am a tropical fish enthusiast and have been for many years. As such, like many with a similar interest, I have long since moved on from a fish tank in the sitting room. Some years ago I converted my garage into a fish breeding house. In my working days, I spent probably two hours a night in there during the week, and several hours over the weekend.

Now I spend slightly more time with my fish – probably 20 hours a week – but I now pursue my hobby with more focus than before. As well as continuing to keep the species which most appeal to me, I particularly concentrate my attention on the species that I know will find ready buyers.

I have a total of 20 aquaria, and at least half of these are set aside purely for breeding and rearing, strictly of species that I know I can be successful with and will command good prices among fellow enthusiasts.

After so many years in the hobby I have a wide range of contacts and friends right across Britain and even on the Continent, so I have no problem disposing of the fish. They may go to individuals, societies, other breeders, shops or wholesalers, and because I have developed a reputation for good quality stock, there is usually a queue of customers.

How did it come about?

It just seemed an obvious thing for me to do, capitalising on my extensive knowledge and my enjoyment of a hobby that has absorbed me for so many years.

Is it working out well for you?

It is working really well for me. I feel incredibly lucky. I am pursuing the all-absorbing hobby that has obsessed me for 30 years and dominated my spare time throughout most of my working years. But now I can not only go to the fish house whenever I like, rather than having to squeeze all the maintenance into evenings and weekends, but I no longer feel I am being self-indulgent and antisocial because I am earning some money for the household. My wife no longer resents all the time I spend splashing about with buckets of water.

And the money?

It is difficult to be precise and, certainly, this does not make me a fortune. But because I specifically set aside the cash I receive from the sale of my fish, it mounts up to something quite worthwhile. I suppose it comes to £2,000 to £3,000 in the course of a year, so it pays for a holiday or two.

The truth is, of course, that it is not all profit – in fact, probably none of it is because the overheads are huge: buying good stock, feeding and maintaining them, light and heat, water, and all the other associated costs. But I have always had these costs in the hobby and would still have them now I have retired, so the breeding programme now pays for the hobby – in my view, at least, it is additional income.

I don't use an accountant and actually I don't declare the income either. It is really small beer and all paid in cash. If I took the trouble to list all the dribs and drabs of income and then listed all the expenses to set against it, I doubt I'd owe the taxman a penny so it's easier not to bother.

PROS:

- Enables me to maintain and even extend a hobby that I love, and in good conscience, too

- Broadened my knowledge and interest in the fish because I have kept and bred species that I may not otherwise have chosen

- Subsidises my pension

- Gives me a focus

- Keeps me in touch with all the friends and contacts that I may otherwise have lost

CONS:

- It's hard work and only worthwhile if you enjoy the hobby side of it

- The financial payback, while useful, probably works out at a pitiful rate compared with the time and effort expended

The gardener

George, 62, formerly a senior local government executive

Why are you still working?

I retired earlier than the statutory retirement age so needed an outlet which I could enjoy and which was completely different from my mainly office-based career. I also needed an extra income to keep me in the style to which I was accustomed.

What are you doing?

I'm a freelance gardener – of the jobbing variety, not serious landscape stuff. I pack my mower and tools into my estate car and set off to create order out of chaos in gardens large and small within a six-mile radius of home. I work several days a week during spring and summer, but less often in winter.

How did it come about?

It had been my hobby for many years, so it seemed sensible to capitalise on something I enjoyed so much. At first I advertised my services, now I get plenty of work through word of mouth. I have built up a reputation, which is very pleasing.

Is it working out well for you?

Very well. I feel very fortunate. I especially value the friendships I make, in particular among the elderly people in sheltered accommodation who are so enthusiastic about gardening. They probably used to be keen gardeners themselves so we like to chat about what's coming up in their communal gardens, and of course it's an opportunity for them to reminisce.

And the money?

It makes up the shortfall between my occupational pension and what I used to earn and it means my wife and I can take holidays without feeling guilty. We roam far and wide through Europe in our camper van.

My accountant's fee is offset against tax. He's priceless because I hate doing the books and I can relax and know everything is in order.

PROS:

- Meeting people
- Being out in the open
- Immeasurable rewards of working with nature and being able to bring pleasure to people

CONS:

- Getting cold, wet and muddy
- Having to go out when I'd rather be sitting in the warm at home with a good book

George makes a very valid point about the pleasure older people get from reminiscing and chatting with him on gardening matters – and it is undoubtedly a mutual pleasure. He presents to them a kindly, reliable, trustworthy face, someone who always turns up at the appointed time and who is never too rushed – or too rude – to stop for a chat. In other words, he is one of those priceless sorts of gardener who everyone you know would willingly entrust their best borders to.

Just trying to find someone to cut the grass on a regular basis can drive some people to thoughts of paving over the whole lot. Where are the wise, characterful, green-fingered types who used to be seen in grandfather's day?

All that's required is someone who doesn't charge a fortune, is trustworthy, nice to have around and will keep coming. Yet how often do you hear the lament 'Well, he came for five weeks and I never saw him again.' An older person, a genuine hobbyist who cuts grass with care and with a passion born of years of interest in the task, is invariably going to be more reliable and display the integrity that merits an entry in the book of treasures.

The photography tutor and cake decorator

Douglas, 73, formerly a bank manager

Why are you still working?

I don't actually need to work. My pension from the bank is just enough to manage on but when I left the bank five months short of my 60th birthday (they 'rationalised' my branch) I commuted some of the pension to fund the building of our present home. There are some funds left from the commutation money to lean on for major purchases like cars and holidays. But I had to last five years before the state pension became available and I wanted to preserve as much of that capital as possible – the older you get the more inflation bites at your capital and the likelier you are to need nursing care – even if only temporarily. So bearing all that in mind, it seemed wise to augment my pension.

What are you doing?

I have continued my hobbies as far as possible, trying to turn them into cost-covering enterprises at least, or even making some money.

Making a liveable wage is problematic, but I know people who make it work as a full-time career, so it should be possible to continue something after normal retirement age.

How did it come about?

The cake icing evolved following reasonable attempts at birthday cakes for the family that emphasised the need for formal training, so I attended classes to learn both royal icing and piping techniques, moving on to flower paste modelling. I joined the local branch of the British Sugarcraft Association, which led to special occasion cakes, even wedding cakes, as I improved. Naturally those attracted a fee, and I was happy enough to cover costs. That has continued since retirement – I do not need to advertise, I get plenty enough to keep me occupied.

As far as photography goes, I had always been fairly good at taking and producing prints and had built a suitable darkroom in the house.

I acquired my Licentiateship of the Royal Photographic Society (RPS) by passing the City and Guilds Photography Diploma (five three-term modules). After about five years I became aware that digital photography had become suitably priced to encourage me to dabble in it. Early attempts were rather poor, although I was not unused to finding my way around computers; the main difficulty was that the standard of the software was quite basic and my photographic requirements were rather higher than the expectations of the public at whom the programs were directed.

Inevitably there was a steep learning curve involved, but I found that I could manage that well enough to help others two or three rungs down the ladder, so I started the digital section in our camera club, often finding myself only a fortnight or so ahead of my 'pupils'. But that has been going on for a good five years now and still continues. I then prepared a six-session course for those who had problems understanding the digital camera handbooks, and ran it at the club for non-members – that raised about £500 for the club (I worked for nothing). Then I was invited by the organisers of an adult education establishment in a nearby town to teach that same course as part of a new venture they were arranging. In turn, that led to another course in digital imaging and I have been running the two courses successfully with minor variations for four years.

A demand from photographic clubs for evening lectures on cameras and imaging has meant the purchase of a digital projector, but its usage cost is being covered in the small fee I have to charge.

On top of that there is an occasional demand for one-to-one tuition, often in my home, because I have acquired the reputation locally of being a useful source of knowledge about digital photography.

Is it working well for you?

The demands on my time from the cake icing and all the various aspects of photography that I'm involved in, including work required for me to obtain my Associateship status with the RPS, mean it is difficult for me to find time to prepare and deliver lessons and presentations.

But photography is a hobby, one that I am very interested in, so it really doesn't count as work.

It is absolutely essential to have a partner who not only keeps the house ticking over smoothly but is prepared to accept that my long hours in front of a computer prevent me sharing the TV programmes she enjoys. And she belongs to the camera club. And she bakes all the cakes!

And the money?

At a rough guess I reckon to make £2.50 per hour on the cake decorating, which is clearly not enough to provide a normal income, but useful to augment spending on the much more expensive photography. The adult education photography courses, for which I was paid £10 an hour and, subsequently, £21 an hour, earned me £2,507 in the last tax year. In all, the teaching work has paid for three new desktop computers, a laptop, three printers, and two monitors, plus a fair amount of up-to-date software. I am capable of managing my own accounts for tax purposes, but that has not been necessary for the tuition courses.

PROS:

- A very useful and often lucrative step beyond an engaging hobby

- Additional cash enables purchase of new equipment, and better holidays

- I am never at a loss for something to do. I have seen men retire who know nothing outside their regular day job, and have no idea how they will fill their time

CONS:

- Time is often at a premium and routine household jobs such as decorating fall by the wayside

- I need to keep careful control of my activities to avoid missing appointments and to ensure I am fully prepared for them. I am as busy after retirement as I seemed to be before, but, hell, it keeps me occupied

Douglas mentions his desire to build up cash reserves in case nursing home fees should need to be paid at any time in the future. He is very wise. It is an unpalatable fact that everyone needs to bear in mind 'the care home syndrome', that uncertain little black cloud that hovers menacingly over the heads of all of us, but is especially threatening to those in their retirement years.

It is common to look upon the capital tied up in your home as the wherewithal for paying the care home bills, should they come in, but it is rarely as cut and dried as that, especially if there is a partner still needing a roof over their head.

It is such a huge commitment, of such an unknown amount and in such a totally unpredictable timescale, that it is quite impossible to second guess. Better, then, to do whatever you can to cover all bases. Build up the nest eggs against the day when, or if, the worst should happen, for care homes can wring your finances dry. Take advice: forewarned is forearmed, so turn to a financial adviser and learn the best way to prepare for what none of us really cares to think about but what is, like it or not, a fact of life. [Find an independent financial adviser near you via **www.unbiased.co.uk**.]

The stone carver

Roderick, 63, formerly a GP

Why are you still working?

I retired at 58 and started an absorbing hobby which has now turned into a means of earning money because there seems to be a market for what I make.

What are you doing?

I work with stone, carving whatever the shape and feel of the stone suggest to me. It could be something abstract or something representational. I spend about 15 hours a week on it, but it is very variable. I feel physically tired after five hours of continuous stone carving.

How did it come about?

My mother-in-law told me about a stonemasons' NVQ Level 1 course in our nearest city and thought I might be interested in it. I enrolled and found that, although I'd had previous experience of woodcarving, I loved stone from the outset.

Is it working out well for you?

Yes. It has achieved enough significance in my life to warrant my building a two-room workshop so that I can carve at home. I anticipate that I will increase the time spent doing it once I have moved into the workshop. I use Hopton Wood (a Derbyshire stone), Forest of Dean sandstone or Portland stone.

And the money?

I have only just got to the stage of selling so it's early days yet. I might ask, say, £450 for a piece that has taken four or five weeks to make. But as my reputation grows, hopefully, I will be able to ask more. It will never be a big money spinner unless I am able to market myself properly and make a name for myself. This is something I need my wife's help with but we will do it because I think we'd both like to see some decent chunks of money coming in so we can splurge a bit on luxuries.

PROS:

- I am excited by the creative processes of discovery, decision-making and producing something
- I enjoy the physicality of stone carving
- It is rewarding to convert an inanimate, amorphous lump of rock into something that has form, interest and hopefully some beauty
- It is satisfying to achieve this without the use of any machinery

CONS:

- Dust
- Occasional back strain

The plant seller

Anne, 65, formerly a journalist and writer

Why are you still working?

I need to supplement my small pension – there's still a mortgage to be paid and there is no question of not occupying myself with something that is rewarding in the sense that I have a small business to develop and something to think about every day. There's also still so much to learn about plants, intellectually and practically.

An important aspect is going out to sell at shows and markets and meeting my customers, many of whom have become friends.

I looked forward to retirement so that I could develop my plant-growing interests and nursery business. I never thought of retirement as stopping work, just a chance to do something that I really enjoyed.

What are you doing?

I grow and sell plants. It is more than a full-time job. My partner (also retired) complains that he's chained to the potting bench all day. Seeds are sown and cuttings taken throughout most of the year. Young plants are also bought in and grown on. Many of these become stock plants and are used as 'mothers' – that is, used to produce young stock from division or cuttings.

I buy in compost-making materials, pots, labels, trays and all the other materials and equipment needed to grow several thousand plants a year. Seed exchanges with other gardeners provide a valuable source of new stock. Some bulbs are grown from seed but most (especially Christmas-flowering hyacinths) are bought wholesale, potted up and on, and sold on. I have a regular weekly plant sale with a co-operative group during the spring, summer and early autumn, specialist plant sales through the early summer and farmers' markets throughout the year. I also get asked to give talks to gardening groups.

Each plant sold has to be accurately labelled with its name, basic growing information, size and price. Loading and labelling two or three hundred plants for travel to a sale can take the best part of a day. Some plants, sold in a good-sized pot for around £3, can take two or three years' care before they are ready to go to a new home, so there's not a huge profit in the business although it is very enjoyable most of the time. Sometimes I wonder, though, when I'm standing in cold drizzly rain with several hundred bulbs to pot up before it gets dark, or when that know-all customer at a sale says to her friend who was just about to buy something: 'Oh, I've got hundreds of those – I'll give you some. Don't buy it!'

Other growers offer the most help. We all learn by experience – where to buy pots and labels, young material, how to display plants, what to charge, how to get on the plant selling circuit, how to keep some sort of basic stock control. If we can help others who are genuinely interested in plants it can only be a good thing. I believe that small nurseries and plant growers do more than anyone to keep some plants going. Garden centres, naturally, have to look for big profits and they'll sell middle-of-the-road popular stuff. But those little gems and harder-to-grow plants come from individuals who do it because they love it.

How did it come about?

Probably because I took A-level Latin at school and became very interested in wild flowers at the same time. The neat classification of plants into family, genus and species, each with a precise name that was at once descriptive and informative, never ceased to amaze me. I grew up with a large garden and took up gardening automatically when I had a house of my own. What was an interest became an absorbing passion and is now a full time occupation.

Although I was in full-time employment as a journalist, I ran a little nursery business in my spare time, selling plants at local markets and seasonal plant fairs and shows.

Is it working out well for you?

It is. From November through to mid-January I tend to lose interest a bit, but that's the time when seeds need to be ordered, shows booked and plans laid for next year. There's a day in January when the year 'turns' and I can't wait for people to start gardening again.

And the money?

It's not hugely profitable. If I ran a nursery open to the public (I don't have the space or the parking or the patience to cope with all the regulations I would have to observe) it would probably make more sense. The outgoings are fairly large but my accountant tells me I make around £6,000 a year which supplements the pension and pays for a few treats – or would if I had time for them.

There are tax implications and I do have a very helpful accountant. I keep every receipt I'm given because it's very easy to forget that even parking charges add up when you're using the car on plant business.

PROS:

• I grow exactly the plants I like and work in my own way

• I enjoy chatting to regular customers, many of whom have become friends. There is a small plant-selling fraternity (or a sorority, perhaps) at the sales who provide a very good support system

• I keep right up to date with what's happening in the plant world and, through suppliers and gardening journals, find out about new plants and planting styles

CONS:

• Keeping plants healthy through summer droughts and alive during cold wet winters

• Becoming weatherbeaten

• Getting up on a cold, sleety morning to unload and set up the stall at 7am, knowing that if the weather doesn't improve I'm going to be standing there freezing and selling virtually nothing for hours on end

The period property restorer

Hans, 53, formerly a prison PE instructor

Why are you still working?

Because it's something I'm really interested in and to provide some spending money for our holiday home in France. It's also nice having some extra cash for frivolous luxuries.

What are you doing?

I work on my own on the restoration of period buildings, doing the actual physical work as well as drawing the plans. I've had plenty of practice doing this as I restored our ancient house in France and our 18th century house in England, which I converted from its derelict state as a former coaching inn.

The work almost always involves me in clambering about in cramped, dark spaces or up ladders, so it's fortunate that I am agile, fit and strong.

I have taken time and trouble to research old building techniques and acquaint myself with, for example, French planning law, so I can be confident I'm not going to land myself or the client in any difficult situations.

Because I work on my own and for myself I can decide how much and when I want to work. One of the fortunate spin-offs of this is that I don't get out of bed very early and for me that's quite important. However, if I give myself a day off in the course of a job I feel very guilty because old work discipline habits die hard.

How did it come about?

Drawing up plans and the actual physical work of house restoration had long been pre-retirement hobbies, so I had guessed it would be something I'd do more of once I had more time on my hands. With both our houses being old there is always something needing to be done. However, I could never have known quite how much my hobbies would expand to shape my life.

While I was working on our Georgian house a neighbour asked me if I could advise him on repair work that he needed to have done on his. Of course, I ended up not just advising him but doing the work for him. While I was up a ladder outside his house I was hailed by the man who runs our local Indian restaurant. Next time we were having a meal in there he came up and asked me if I'd have a look at some fairly extensive work that needed doing after a leak in the roof had badly damaged the period features in an upstairs room.

And so it went on, the requests for my specialist services increasing through word of mouth.

Is it working out well for you?

Very much so. I get huge satisfaction from my work environment, which is in great contrast to my previous one. All I have to do now is to learn to say 'No' to ensure I keep work to a part-time activity.

And the money?

It varies from job to job, obviously, but if I work just five days a month it brings my income up to the same level as my final salary pre-retirement.

PROS:

- Fewer bars than when I worked in the prison service – and more fresh air
- Earning money through something I enjoy so much
- Finding I can make such profitable use of what were once 'hobby' skills
- Meeting good people who share my passion for restoring and preserving beautiful buildings

CONS:

- Having to keep records of income and expenditure, but I'm learning. Fortunately, my daughter-in-law is a chartered accountant and she has wagged a warning finger at me about cash transactions

Chapter 8

Fulfilling a dream

Happiness and contentment almost inevitably result from being free to do what we want. And if that 'want' has been around for a long time, maybe nurtured over many years until retirement released it from its straitjacket, then the pleasure is all the greater. So it is with a dream, a vision of how life could be, if only …

With retirement comes that longed-for opportunity, as well as the time and the motivation, to fly those kites.

Some people close up their houses and disappear abroad to scratch the itch of the travel bug, but others have aspirations that keep their feet more firmly on home ground.

Pursuing a dream, mostly seen as a preserve of the young, is probably more difficult in many ways when you are older. For one thing, the energy of youthful enthusiasm is no longer there. In its place is the wisdom, and a little cynicism perhaps, that comes from a life well lived – along with, it has to be said, a touch of the 'Can I be bothered?' the nagging little affliction that can trouble the weary retiree.

Ambivalence, where dreams are concerned, means they stay just that. Bringing them to reality requires a belief in yourself and your abilities. It also needs commitment – the sort that can drive you from a standing start to full dream-working mode without being deterred by the odd speed hump along the way.

The bookshop owners

Rashid, 61, formerly a Post Office supervisor, and Alison, 60, a special needs teacher

Why are you still working?

We'd always planned to do this, to retire before we got too doddery and run a bookshop. We dreamed about it from when we first found that we both loved books, which was probably on our first date when we were at teacher training college.

What are you doing?

We own and run a bookshop in the market town where we have lived since retiring from our respective careers five years ago. It took us nearly three years to find and secure the right premises, and during that time we both worked in other people's bookshops to learn about the trade and to keep the finances ticking over.

It is very hard work – probably much harder than we had ever imagined. You have to be really proactive and move with the times in this business or you'll go under fast. For instance, we have had to become red hot with technology because a lot of the business involves using a computer and we can't keep calling on professional help when things go wrong because we can't afford that, either in time or money. So we've become our own techie troubleshooters and it has made a big difference.

Anyone in retail these days is at risk from being undercut by both internet retailing and big name multiples, and nowhere more so than in the book business. Independent bookshops like ours are in competition with Amazon for a start, supermarkets with their huge markdowns on price, and the chain bookstores that offer deals like three for the price of two. Because we can't compete on price we have to offer something more – a lot more, such as a book club, a second hand section, wall space for local artists, children's reading sessions, author appearances, gift wrapping, themed evenings, poetry readings, you name it we throw ourselves into it.

Early dreams of running a bookshop featured visions of us both sitting reading to our hearts' content. I don't know when I last picked up a book to read it! It just isn't like that. There is always something to be done, which is good because it shows we are busy and successful.

There is always room for improvement and we are constantly looking at ways to build the business. There's no time to stand still.

How did it come about?

Through our own determination. There were times when we might have given up, especially when we thought we'd found the perfect shop premises and someone else sneaked in and gazumped us.

It helps having a dream – a realisable one – and keeping that in mind when things threaten to send you off balance.

My first career was as a primary school teacher and Alison was in special needs teaching, so we are OK with children, which surprisingly is quite important in a bookshop. They're your next generation of customers so they must be well looked after.

Is it working out well for you?

It is. We would happily shut up shop between mid-January and mid-March each year because business is so poor, but apart from that period we have no complaints. This year we're planning to take a holiday, our first, and will employ a retired bookseller and his wife to run the shop. I think this will be good for us. The work is varied and it's brought out different strengths in both of us. It's interesting to see how much we have both learnt and evolved since embarking on this, at the very time we might otherwise have been running our batteries down and doing nothing with our lives.

And the money?

You don't get rich in this business but you do get great job satisfaction from working among books and meeting such a great lot of customers, nearly all of whom are as passionate about books as we are.

Our intention is to go on building up the business while we're still enjoying it, and then we'll look to sell it in about five or six years' time. That's when the question about money will become more relevant – not now!

PROS:

- Great job satisfaction
- Meeting so many nice enthusiastic customers
- Owning our own business that we have grown from scratch
- A sense of achievement
- Seeing our dream come true

CONS:

- The worry of owning the business – it never goes away
- Difficult customers – not many, but they linger in the memory
- You don't have many allies
- So little time to read

The artist

Andrew, 62, formerly an architect

Why are you still working?

I need the income. I would also hate doing nothing and I feel a vocation to fulfil my long-held desire to paint.

What are you doing?

Since I retired at 56 I have been doing watercolour painting of landscapes, townscapes and still lifes. I also help in running a small art gallery in Hampton Court together with an artists' co-operative (my partner Liz owns the gallery). I aim to work a four-day week.

How did it come about?

I didn't intend to retire but had become disillusioned with the world of architecture as I was experiencing it. There seemed to be so much legislation to stifle creativity.

I always wanted to paint and knew I had the talent. Meeting Liz enabled me to pursue this with a degree of financial security. Together we bought and renovated the gallery. This provided a showcase for my work. Later on, the artists' co-operative idea developed to enable me to spend more time painting and less time running the gallery.

Is it working out well for you?

Yes, better than I could have imagined in terms of lifestyle and happiness. Financially, I could not do without some private pension back-up but things are improving as I get better known.

And the money?

At the moment I am making between £4,000 and £6,000 a year from this work, which goes towards general living expenses.

Painting is a very volatile business and is highly sensitive to general economic climate. I am trying to find more commercial ways of promoting my work through, say, postcards and small booklets, but not being naturally commercial-minded this is difficult for me. We receive an income from the artists using the gallery, which is divided between myself and my partner. I also take drawdown from a small private pension.

Our excellent accountant manages to lump my work and the gallery together to facilitate maximum tax allowances. Careful records have to be kept of all materials, expenditure and so on.

PROS:

• I really enjoy what I'm doing. I couldn't be happier doing anything else, I am quite sure of that

CONS:

• Inevitably having to make money from painting means that there is some tension between merely being creative, doing what I want, and being commercial. I am still learning how to balance this: for example, I am currently doing a number of commissions for local people of their houses which I do not really like doing as I am not choosing the subject and how it is presented. Inevitably they wish for pet dogs and pot plants!

The bric-a-brac seller

Peggy, 68, formerly worked voluntarily for a charity

Why are you still working?

For 25 years I worked in a voluntary capacity, but virtually full-time, running a local branch of an international charity. I did everything, from locating shop premises and recruiting volunteer staff to storing, mending and cleaning items handed in for sale.

I retired from my charity work at the age of 60 due to poor health – my husband's and my own. I felt unable to cut back to a minor role after so many years in a major one, so I decided to call it a day.

I have always been a busy person – raising children, helping with grandchildren, helping with my husband's business, doing my charity work, so to suddenly find myself drowned in leisure time was a shock to the system.

I actually became terribly depressed and felt I was drifting into old age without a whimper. Money wasn't especially tight but I was bored and unhappy.

What are you doing?

I run a modest bric-a-brac stall (I like to think of it as an antiques business but I realise its true scale). I have rented a stall in a local twice-weekly antiques market and I have become a shopkeeper. I have always had a great interest in bits and pieces with some history to them, and although I would not profess to have any great specialist knowledge, I believe I have an eye for what's good and what isn't. I also know plenty of people whose brains I can pick if I'm ever in doubt.

I suppose it was always a dream that one day I should run a little antiques shop somewhere, but I thought that had long passed me by. So this is, if you like, a dream come partly true – but on a very small scale.

How did it come about?

My children were increasingly concerned about my low spirits after my husband and I retired from all our commitments and moved to a smaller house. They could see how depressed I was. So they hatched this plan about the stall, knowing I could probably do the work without overstretching myself physically or mentally and that I wouldn't be abandoning my husband for long each time I went out. We checked out the cost of the stall – almost a token payment, really – and set about collecting up stock. Quite a bit came from my own cupboards where I had hoarded things I liked over the years, then we had great fun combing car boot sales and second-hand shops to gather up more.

Is it working out well for you?

It has worked wonderfully well for four years so far. I've made lots of new friends and acquaintances and it's put a lot of fun and interest into my life. It has raised my spirits no end.

And the money?

If I'm honest, I don't think I've made much money, especially if you set that against the hours I put in, but money was never the main driving force for me. Most of my stock sells for just a few pounds at most; it's very rare for anything to carry a three figure price tag. I suppose that most weeks I make an average of £50 to £100 profit over the two days, and some weeks I can even lose if I fail to cover the £28 rent.

There are costs involved in buying stock and the petrol needed for getting around.

But more than money is the excitement that rewards you if you find something that you know is going to sell for a lot more than you've paid for it. You can't put a price on that feeling. It's happened once, so far, when I sold a small pair of very old Steiff teddy bears to a collector for an awful lot more than they'd cost me. Lovely! But it's swings and roundabouts. The next day I just about broke even.

The thing is, if I wanted to make more money I probably could, but I'd have to devote more time to it and I don't want to do that. I like it just the way it is.

PROS:

- It has been so uplifting for my morale
- I've made new friends
- The little bit of extra money, which is always welcome

- It's brought something completely new to my life at an age when I had never thought it could or would happen.

- It has helped my husband see me in a different light. I'd always played a central role in the family and in my voluntary work, but that contribution had been taken for granted. Now I'm doing something in my own right and I think I've earned a new respect. My husband is very supportive and as helpful as he can be. It's good for us both

CONS:

- Sometimes it takes a bit of an effort to brave winter cold or rain to load up the car and drive off to set up my stall, knowing that few customers will be likely to call in

- Sometimes I worry about leaving my husband at home alone, but I have my 'senile mobile' with me so we can keep in touch while I'm out

The grape picker

George, 63, formerly an airport security officer

Why are you still working?

To augment my modest pension and to ensure that my partner and I can live the sort of life we dreamed of for so long. This is what we talked of doing for ages. We have moved from the north-west of England to rural Italy, near my grandfather's birthplace, and we are renting a tiny house before deciding exactly where we want to settle. In the meantime we live a simple life: we keep our expenses to a minimum, which is easier here than in England because we can grow so much of our food, and when we've saved up enough we take off from time to time in our camper van to explore Europe, sometimes for months at a time.

What are you doing?

Since moving to Italy 18 months ago I've been working in a variety of ways. Some of it is seasonal work: grape picking through the early autumn, olive picking through the rest of autumn and into the winter, and I also keep an eye on Brits' holiday houses when they're unoccupied, I'm project managing the reconstruction of a house for an absentee owner, and with my partner we cater for private parties – something we used to do before we moved.

Is it working out well for you?

It's wonderful. I've no complaints at all. We have the best of all worlds – a better climate than England's being one of the major benefits. But we appreciate how much more simply life can be lived over here and this suits us economically as well as spiritually.

At first I wasn't sure how I would cope with the physical demands of the outdoor work because some of the olive groves are on incredibly steep slopes. But I surprised myself by getting used to it quite quickly; in fact I have seen off many younger men as they've found the going too tough and given up. It is very hard physically, added to which you have the sun beating down on you – or sometimes rain, of course.

The camaraderie is great and the friendly chatter has helped expand my Italian vocabulary in all sorts of interesting ways.

As far as the other work is concerned, it is less onerous but still has to be carefully planned. You have to bear in mind you're carrying quite a responsibility by caring for someone's home in their absence so you must be organised and keep in good contact with the owners. They're paying me to give them peace of mind, basically. I cut the grass where necessary, give the places a good airing before the owners come out, and of course check security when there's no one around. I've dealt with two hornets' nests and a wasps' nest so far, as well as becoming a dab hand at freeing jammed shutters.

The project management is more hassle than I would have expected. Fortunately I speak good Italian so I don't have a problem communicating with the builders. I think they appreciate this and we get along fine, but it was a bit prickly in the early stages as they probably thought I was a spy in the camp. I'd had some experience before when I oversaw the building of two extensions to our old home about 20 years ago, so I was aware of some of the hitches that can occur. It's all progressing well, so I feel pretty chuffed with myself for that.

We only do the catering on a very small scale, mainly for friends or friends of friends. My partner worked as a chef so she does all the creative stuff while I act as the gopher. I like it as you get to work in other people's homes and you learn more and more about Italy and the Italians – two endlessly fascinating subjects!

And the money?

The money in no way reflects the amount of effort I put in, but that's not the whole reason I work. For instance, I am paid €50 (approx £35) a day for grape and olive picking – and the day lasts from 7.30am to 7pm with a couple of hours' break for lunch. It's the most tiring way I could imagine of earning money, but beggars can't be choosers in this rural community.

The other work brings in odd amounts which probably total about €250 (approx £160) a month, in a good month that is.

It's all what they call 'black money' in Italy: in other words, the taxman doesn't know.

PROS:

• It's a privilege to work with good people in any job, but working the land in Italy has taught me some important life lessons. It is humbling to see how hard people work and it makes me quite guilty when I recall how I used to complain about long days when I was in airport security. A long day sitting down is very different from a long day of physical labour in all weathers

- I am fitter and healthier than I've ever been before, even as a young man

- I am playing a part in the life of our community, contributing in a small way to its vitality as one season moves into another

- I've proved to myself that I can adapt to testing situations, and that's given me quite a boost after a working life where I was hardly stretched at all, mentally or physically

CONS:

- I really can't think of any, other than the fact that the outdoor work plays hell with my hands. But who cares?

Chapter 9

The portfolio lifestyle – such a flexible friend

What could be nicer than a mixed bag of goodies – a little bit of this, a little bit of that? It's a work/life concept that is becoming increasingly common. Two or three days a week, perhaps, work part-time in some capacity or other then a bit of jobbing DIY or grass-cutting or jam-making on a self-employed basis, a few hours of voluntary work and a healthy dose of leisure time, too. It reads like a recipe for a long and contented life.

As you've possibly been one of the pioneers of job flexibility throughout your working life – something that Baby Boomers perfected – you could well apply the same principles to your retirement and carve out a portfolio lifestyle.

It was back in the 1980s that the business management guru Charles Handy predicted such a shift in work patterns, forecasting that people would run parallel jobs rather than sequential ones. In his ground-breaking book, *The Age of Unreason* (1989), Handy explored the work culture in a rapidly changing world and coined the term 'portfolio worker' for someone earning a living from a number of different sources (as in a share portfolio) independent of one organisation. Now his prediction is proving true for those who work in retirement, too. They find that mixing a variety of jobs with other pastimes and periods of relaxation can be both pleasurable and fulfilling.

Portfolio working is a creative way to ply your skills – not just, or not even, the ones you have used throughout your career. Just because you have been a master baker all your working life doesn't mean you have to go on trying to earn money with flour, yeast and water once you've retired.

These are some of the aspects of the creative, pick-and-mix portfolio lifestyle that will help you determine if it's the route you want to take:

- You decide how much work and how much leisure you want in your week
- Not all your sources of income are dependent on one job – the risk is spread
- It has an appeal for time management experts
- There is no time to be bored
- Variety helps maintain interest
- Great choice and opportunity
- You choose how your life is structured
- You must be highly organised

An employer with two part-time members of staff who fit their work in with another couple of part time jobs each, says she has always been impressed by how organised and dedicated they are. She had feared there might be some conflict of interest, or certainly some confusion at times, but there has been no sign of any difficulty. The only drawback she can think of is the dilemmas both the women face in the run-up to Christmas when office parties tend to clash.

Portfolio lifestyle 1

Tom, 71, formerly the managing director of the UK affiliate of an international company

Why are you still working?

To make a contribution, to give something back and to be occupied mentally and physically so that I get up and out of the house.

What are you doing?

I have put together a variety of work, some paid, some unpaid, and it certainly keeps me on my toes.

My activities are these:

1 Film extra: I signed up a few months ago with two agencies and so far have done two films – one of five days and the other of one day. There is an awful lot of hanging around so it can be very boring and pretty depressing when it's cold and wet. I wouldn't recommend it, to be honest. It has very few redeeming features but there are some interesting people to chat with and there's time to get on with my reading.

2 Business mentor for the Prince's Youth Business Trust, which loans money to young people who can't get it from banks to start small businesses.

3 I spend about two days a week recruiting volunteers for the British Charitable Consultancy Trust (BCCT) and British Executive Service Overseas (BESO) development charity, which sends expert volunteers abroad on short-term assignments to the Third World. I have been doing this for about seven years. It involves searching their database by skill/experience and inviting likely candidates to consider an assignment. Considerable follow-up involvement is required if the two sides reach an agreement. I work from London, so the volunteers travel to me.

4 Help the Hospices is an umbrella charity for the UK and internationally and I do one to two days a week doing administrative dogsbody jobs. It's unpaid but they will cover the cost of my lunch.

5 Shareholder Partnership [www.sharepartner.com] finds people who have unclaimed assets and helps them recover them. I recently started as a consultant and, while the future here is uncertain, it could be interesting.

6 My wife and I are Friends of Highgate Cemetery and I usually do one afternoon each week on the East Gate collecting the entrance fee and directing visitors.

How did it come about?

1 I found one film extras agency in the local paper and I learnt about the other while I was involved in the first film.

2, 3 and 4 Found through REACH, the agency that puts professional people seeking work in touch with charities seeking help [www.reach-online.org.uk 020 7582 6543].

5 Found via the internet.

6 Through membership of the Friends of Highgate Cemetery.

Is it working out well for you?

Like the curate's egg – good in parts.

And the money?

1 Film extras are paid about £80/100 day.

2 Voluntary and unpaid.

3 At the beginning I was paid £50 a day (about £1,500 a year) and then when BESO merged with Voluntary Service Overseas I worked there for a little while longer and earned £13,000 for eight months' work. I now work for BCCT, which replaced BESO, for a small commission on assignments.

4 Voluntary.

5 I am paid commission on results – but as yet I have earned nothing.

6 I earn nothing for this – it is voluntary, but enjoyable, and adds something to the pot pourri of activity.

PROS:

- Keeps me occupied and my brain active
- Interesting variety
- A little extra money
- My diary is always full

CONS:

- The work isn't terribly challenging
- My diary is always full

Portfolio lifestyle 2

Ian, 57, formerly in public relations, and Stella, 55, formerly an IT manager

Why are you still working?

We decided to leave our jobs because we were both disenchanted with life in this country and we thought we might move to Portugal, where we'd owned a holiday home for four years. We knew that wherever we lived we would have to work in some way to earn money and it has turned out that it's easier for us to do that in this country than overseas. Our thoughts of moving are therefore on hold while we are so busy.

What are you doing?

We're doing a lot, working very hard in fact, but because it doesn't involve either of us in putting on a suit and travelling to an office every day, it doesn't really seem like work as we used to know it.

When we walked away from our jobs we had enough money to see us through the first year while we drew breath and looked around to see what we might like to do. It wasn't as irresponsible as it might seem because we had paid off our mortgage and we had the house in Portugal as collateral. Owning two houses outright does give you a certain amount of courage.

1 **Letting the house.** Within a month we had received inquiries from two lots of friends wanting to rent our holiday house. As this would bring in a serious lump of money we abandoned plans to spend a lazy summer in the Portuguese sun and decided to market the house properly as a holiday let. This meant we had to remove all our personal belongings and spruce up the house to meet the sort of standards people expect when they're paying £1,000 a week in high season. It hurt a bit, de-personalising and sanitising it so much, but seeing the house in a new light as a commercial proposition and our passport to a different way of life helped us keep our focus.

We built a website, registered with a couple of internet letting agencies, advertised locally and nationally, and before long the bookings were rolling in. Many of our guests are returning for a second or third time, which is lovely.

If we want to go out there, which we quite often do, then we just block off those periods on the letting calendar.

Running a holiday property from a distance is a real worry. You have to have somebody on the spot who you can trust and who deals with all the cleaning, the house and garden maintenance, any emergencies that might crop up (lost keys, a blocked loo, that sort of thing) and who will liaise with us back in England. We had a couple of false starts but now we have someone we're very happy with.

2 **Building websites.** This is something that developed from the website we created for our own holiday house. One or two people complimented us on it and we got them to pass on the word that we were in the market to take commissions, and we were also proactive in selling our services to other homeowners in Portugal who were looking to let their properties. It is a modest-sized business, but it has all grown from that. We advertise in a specialist magazine but otherwise rely on word of mouth.

Between us, we probably spend about two or three days a month not just building websites for other people but maintaining them too, plus the hour or two needed to keep our own up to date.

Obviously, a good broadband link is vital for that and we're lucky that we are both very IT literate.

3 **Importing goods.** We have Portuguese friends who run a small pottery and we import some of their terracotta tableware to three shops in England. This is something that we feel we could develop and we're looking at other items, such as textiles or prints, that we could add. We think there's a market, we just need to be sure we want, or need, to go down this route. At the moment it's on a very small scale – we simply bring a few packing cases of tableware back in the van with us when we've done a furniture delivery (see below). It takes little time and effort on our part when we're simply acting as the middle man.

4 **Furniture delivery.** We recognised a gap in the market for small loads of furniture and household goods to be delivered from the UK to Portugal. Again, we advertised in a specialist magazine and put the word round among some of the expat communities in Portugal. We get one or two inquiries every couple of months

and these result in about three bookings a year. This suits us perfectly because it means we're not away too often and we can utilise the empty van on the way back for other people's part loads and the tableware that we import.

We always travel together. It can be tough going, depending on the weather and the time of year, but we share the driving and we enjoy discovering parts of Portugal we didn't know before. The van is hired so we don't have the expense of maintaining one.

5 **Selling property.** Again through Portuguese friends, who have an estate agency in the Algarve, we act as the UK arm of their business by publicising their properties for sale and introducing prospective clients from the UK. We get 2% on any sales that result. We're the facilitators, and having bought a house and done business in Portugal ourselves, and being able to speak the language reasonably well, we're well placed to help and advise UK purchasers. We have our own website for this side of our work and we advertise nationally.

How did it come about?

One thing has evolved from another. Things just seem to have happened – through someone approaching us or through us seeing where a few pounds could be made and built up into something more substantial. The key to it all, obviously, was the fact we already had a foothold in Portugal and we have gradually capitalised on that. Being able to speak the language has definitely been an advantage.

Is it working out well for you?

It's really good. If we wanted to we could step up a gear but we have no great desire to do that. Our lives are busy but not in a frantic, head-banging way like before, and we can escape almost as often as we wish, if necessary taking some of our work, like the website building and maintenance, with us. As long as we have internet access we can function, wherever we are.

And the money?

Not great, but for the amount of work we do and the time it entails, it certainly beats our previous existence. The holiday lets bring in the major part – about £14,000 a year, but we have considerable expenses to pay out of that, such as all the utility bills and the housekeeper. We probably clear about £10,000.

All our activities, added together, bring us a total annual income of about £20,000. It's not possible to break down how much each part of our portfolio earns us because it varies so much from month to month and year to year.

Some of it, like the furniture delivery, we make very little on, probably no more than £200-£300 a trip, but we like doing it and using the empty van on the return trip makes economic sense. The property selling venture blows hot and cold but it's better to be involved than not as the chance is always there to make money.

Website charges are based on our time and expertise and can vary from £200 for something very basic and simple to several thousand for something that sings and dances and needs a lot of maintenance.

PROS:

- We have a lifestyle of our choice that we've built together from a standing start
- There is scope for more work and income if we want
- We work together
- It is good for us to live within modest means – it's enriching in many ways
- We're much more interesting people than we used to be

CONS:

- Having to pay an accountant – it's a devil of a job keeping track of everything anyway, but he knows the system and we trust him entirely to do the best for us

Portfolio lifestyle 3

James, 71, formerly head of employment for a government department

Why are you still working?

I was in the armed services for 38 years so I was never going to be idle if I could help it. I enjoy new challenges and making a contribution to society in as many ways as I can.

What are you doing?

Quite a lot, but basically it breaks down into one major area of full-time work for which I get paid and a number of other activities which are unpaid. Together, they make up a busy and varied lifestyle that seems to suit me.

1 My main area of employment is as an independent freelance expert witness in personal injury cases, working with occupational psychologists on producing employment skills reports. To keep totally on top of my subject I have to attend regular legal updates and tutorials and conduct an ongoing research programme in skills and employment. This ensures I'm at the top of my tree and can remain working full-time – and charge four-figure fees for each instruction. I have qualified to be accredited by the Law Society and to gain membership of the Academy of Experts as an expert witness.

2 I also work part-time and unpaid with SSAFA (Soldiers, Sailors, Airmen and Families' Association) Forces Help.

3 I'm governor of a large comprehensive school.

4 I'm on the executive of two county council education committees.

How did it come about?

My full-time work is a direct result of my last job, from which I retired at the age of 65. As head of employment for a government department many people had looked to me for advice and so after I left I was approached to continue as an adviser to the firm which had been awarded the department's private commercial contract by the government.

The preparation of employment skills reports for personal injury cases grew from the annual research programme in skills and employment that I had to conduct for this firm.

The rest of my 'work' came about by being asked or, in the case of my involvement with SSAFA Forces Help, it came through REACH [**www.reach-online.org.uk** 020 7582 6543], the organisation that matches retirement skills and vacancies.

I had done some work through REACH before, doing part-time expenses-only marketing for an academic charitable organisation which trains people to run briefing sessions for those about to retire. I left that in order to train and work one day a week as an adviser for the Citizens Advice Bureau, but after two and a half years I decided to volunteer to use my experience as a caseworker with SSAFA Forces Help, becoming the county secretary and co-ordinating the countywide function of the national charity.

Is it working out well for you?

It's most satisfactory. I feel that my experience in both the paid and voluntary sectors has shown the value of networking and being willing to adapt. Meeting people and developing a network really is easier than it seems.

Every contact which one makes may have another contact which is interesting and productive. One thing leads to another if you look for it.

The community is full of open doors for people who wish to do things, but you have to be prepared to watch and learn, be trained, be flexible and keep your counsel until you know how you can contribute your skills. You aren't expected to know everything but the bit you do know can be valuable.

And the money?

My income doubles my retirement pension but unfortunately attracts tax at 40%. I engage and pay an accountant annually.

PROS:

- Variety
- Being kept busy, active and mentally alert
- Hopefully making the best use of my life skills
- Bringing in some useful extra money to the home

CONS:

- The diary is nearly always full

Portfolio lifestyle 4

Steve, 58, formerly a teacher and department head

Why are you still working?

Because I can! I also need the money to pay the mortgage. But I want to work and don't necessarily regard 'retirement' as not working. It's more of an opportunity to transfer skills accrued from previous work and which now allow me to have a little more control over what I do and when I do it.

What are you doing?

1 I play music/sing/entertain on the hotel cabaret circuits, which I've been doing for 40 years. I work about three nights a week. I put a lot of effort into this because it has to be slick and professional.

2 I'm a qualified massage therapist, a qualification I studied for after escaping from teaching. I work from home and also visit clients. I love doing this and am currently undertaking another course on seated acupressure massage to enable me to work more on site, in offices and shops. I see about eight clients a week.

3 I work as a publicity/information officer for a small national charity involved with the deaf community. I do two days in the office and a half day at home.

4 I work as a marker for a couple of examination boards. This is just once a year, between April and June. It's incredibly tedious but pays for my foreign travel.

5 I work for a couple of distribution companies who get the contracts to distribute Yellow Pages and phone books. They employ me as a team leader and I recruit/persuade people to deliver routes – some local, some in the middle of nowhere. This happens between September and November.

How did it come about?

I've never just done one thing – my boredom threshold is too low – so these things have evolved over time. It has to be said, though, and I'm not wishing to sound conceited here, that I'm lucky in that I am quite good at several things, had a good education, come from a middle class family and my teaching experience gave me good people skills as well as a lot of self-confidence and motivation.

I might not be typical and I think there may well be a sociological perspective here – those who have … and so on. Also, my two children have left home so I can exploit the freedom that comes with that situation.

Is it working out well for you?

I can't think of any other way of organising my life at the moment although I know that will change because I'm always changing things.

Some people say, 'Yes, well, it's OK for you,' and I know I am lucky in what I *can* do, but ultimately it's about attitude and probably about knowing what you *don't* want to do before you can feel good about something else.

A lot of people I know also look for jobs which pay the same sort of rate as the job they want to escape or change. They overlook the fact that doing this will probably result in them being subjected to the same sort of pressures and stresses as their current job. You need to make a lifestyle change for it to work.

And the money?

I have a pension from teaching, which I took early. I spent most of the lump sum and the monthly income now covers my mortgage and a few other things. It's not really enough to live the sort of life I need at the moment but it's a good bolster.

I probably earn more than £20,000 from the work I do but if I don't I always feel there will be another way of earning something. You have to believe that, and in yourself, to do these things.

Self-assessment for tax purposes is very easy – you don't need to waste money on paying someone to do that. I don't save much on the grounds that I might not get the chance to spend it.

PROS:

- Freedom

- The chance to diversify

- Opportunity to meet people from all walks of life

- Staying in bed if I want

- No attainment targets or schemes of work (did I ever do those?).

- Generally feeling that I do have choice and a lot more control over my life

CONS:

- Self-employment can be tricky – you often have to actively seek work

- Working from home can give a feeling of isolation – you need to network

- I often have periods where I earn lots of money and then lean periods – I have to manage this with care and I'm not brilliant at accounts

Portfolio lifestyle no. 5

Sheila, 58, formerly a theatre wardrobe mistress

Why are you still working?

I would go mad with boredom if I didn't do something. My husband is still working, and says he intends to go on until his colleagues carry him out feet first, so I want to keep busy too. There's nothing to keep me tied to the house all day. Since I was compulsorily retired, made redundant, call it what you will, two years ago I have managed to piece together several activities in the areas of life which interest me.

What are you doing?

1 I'm a steward for the National Trust at the big house and gardens close to where we live. This is seasonal work, April to October, plus more if I want it around Christmas when the shop opens. I enjoy it very much and would like to do more than my present 12 hours a week if the opportunity arises.

2 I make jams and chutneys for the Country Market stall that my fellow producers and I run at farmers' markets around the area. A couple of us man the stall, taking it in turns on a rota basis, so that side of it isn't too onerous as my turn only comes up every couple of months, but it's a whole team of us who work on producing all the things that are sold. We work in our respective homes, which have to meet strict health and safety requirements and be regularly inspected. This aspect is rather irksome and may yet cause me to give up, but that would be a shame because I like gathering all the ingredients from my garden and the hedgerows and then turning it into preserves. The fact I have this outlet through which I can sell it is a bonus.

3 I run the wardrobe for our local amateur operatic society – with some help. I've done it for years but have been able to devote more time to it since leaving work and I really enjoy it. There's quite a lot involved and some of the costumes require a great deal of care in their handling and storage. There's always loads of mending and patching to be done, too, and I could be busy with that almost every day of the week if I wasn't doing other things as well.

4 I work all day Friday and Saturday mornings at a costume hire shop. They are the busiest times but I like that, it gives me a buzz. I always look forward to going there and meeting all our lovely customers and sorting out their outfits. I also do a bit of mending, paid on a piecework basis, for Lisa, who owns the business,

but this is more as a favour than a serious money earner. She and I used to work together years ago. When possible, I take the mending home.

5 I'm a volunteer helper with the Riding for the Disabled Association (RDA). I give as much time as I can, doing everything from making mugs of tea to cleaning out the stables, depending on where the help is needed most when I happen to be there. I do at least half a day a fortnight – and it's never enough.

6 Every Monday and Wednesday morning I spend an hour, between about 8am and 9am, with my elderly neighbour, just keeping her company really, but I usually end up doing a spot of ironing or something else while we talk.

How did it come about?

1 I answered an advertisement in our local paper. We've been National Trust members for years and I had always been curious to know what being a steward involved. The interview process was far from gruelling, but obviously they wanted to be sure of my bona fides and my reliability.

2 Through a friend who makes pastries and pies for the same Country Market group – they're all over the country and used to be known as Women's Institute Markets.

3 Both my daughters belonged to the operatic society and this work is a legacy of my involvement through them all those years ago.

4 My friend Lisa wanted me to go in with her when she started the costume hire business five years ago but I wasn't keen as I was happy at the theatre, so she did it alone. As soon as she knew I was in the market for work she offered me whatever hours I wanted, which was very kind. She didn't even give me a

chance to find out what it was like to be retired and put my feet up!

5   I have a grandson who is autistic and he is taken riding once a week with his classmates from the special unit at school. It has made such an amazing difference to him and I feel that doing the little I do to help is my way of saying 'Thank you'. As a family we also do some fund-raising for the RDA and my daughter is on the committee.

6   We've been neighbours of this lady since we moved here 33 years ago. I've been visiting her on a regular basis since her husband died 18 months ago. I know that other people from the village go in to see her too, and I'm sure they find her as rewarding as I do.

Is it working out well for you?

Very well. I am probably even busier now than when I was working full-time, but without the pressure. I feel very privileged to have so many good things going on in my life.

And the money?

1   The stewarding is about £6.25 an hour, so I get about £75 a week through the summer.

2   Obviously this depends on how much of my produce sells, and my overheads are considerable when weighed against the maximum one can reasonably ask for a pot of jam. But I probably clear an average of about £20 a market and there are five a month.

3   This is voluntary.

4   I get £120 for my one and a half days, plus £6 for repairing a costume, assuming it isn't too complicated or time consuming.

5 and 6   Both these are voluntary.

PROS:

- Variety – there's something different every day
- It all keeps my brain and my body active
- Nice to be useful and wanted
- No time to start feeling old
- A little bit of extra spending money
- Gives me plenty to talk about

CONS:

- Nothing – no complaints at all

Chapter 10

Odd jobs

A little of what you fancy does you good – a hoary old expression but one that could certainly be said to apply to the sort of casual, part-time work that many retired people like to do. It may not be physically or mentally demanding but it enables them to earn some money, have an interest in the outside world, keep active and get out of the home. This latter can perhaps best be translated, in many cases, as 'out from under my wife's/husband's feet'.

Certainly for Ann, whose husband, Bob, a hospital car driver, is featured later in this chapter, getting out of the house keeps their relationship lively and gives them both plenty to talk about when they are together. "We'd have very dull lives if we didn't both get out to do a bit of work," she says.

Ann is 69 and works as a school cleaner. She loves it: the routine, the companionship, the work itself and, above all, being appreciated for it. She says: "They've told me they never want me to leave. It's a nice feeling to know I'm so wanted."

The working hours impose a routine on her life – out of the front door on the dot of 2.45pm every weekday and home again at 5.15pm. By the time she's home, Bob is back from his day's work. They relax and then have their evening meal before walking into town to do another cleaning job, this time at the bookmaker's. They work together on this one. "We don't have time for anything silly like arguments," Ann says "We're always busy and that suits us. If he was moping round the house all the time he'd drive me mad."

Turning your hand to something relatively unchallenging does have its attractions, especially if it follows a working life of stress, pressure, travel, targets and burdensome responsibility. A spot of carefree shelf stacking at Tesco can seem very alluring, and many do indeed take that route.

Perhaps it is one of B&Q's distinctive orange uniforms that attracts. B&Q were pioneers in employing older people – not because they felt sorry for them but because they had very tight targets on reducing staff turnover. Youngsters would join, get a full training and six months later they'd get bored and go off and do something else.

In contrast, employ a keen-to-work batch of 55 year olds and they're not going to come in late because they've been out clubbing the night before, they're not going to come in with a hangover – or they're less likely to, at least – and they're not going to phone in sick because their girlfriend's dumped them and they're in tears.

As long ago as 1989 B&Q opened a store in Macclesfield that was staffed entirely by men and women aged 50-plus. The results showed what a good move this was. Compared with other B&Q stores:

- Profits were 18% higher
- Staff turnover was six times lower
- Short term absenteeism dropped by 60%
- Customer perception of service improved
- Skill base of the workforce increased

Since then, and through developing its over-50s recruitment policy, nearly a quarter of B&Q's total workforce of 57,000 are aged 50 or over.

Customers, as those figures above clearly show, seem to think they're getting a better deal when the workforce is older. They tend to be more inclined to seek out a more mature member of staff when wanting DIY advice, for example. If you need help with something in the home maintenance and DIY line, you are inevitably going to turn to someone who at least looks as though they've banged a nail into a piece of wood a few times in their life.

Also recognising the value of an older workforce and wanting to meet the challenge of an ageing population, Sainsbury's started developing plans as early as 1986 by targeting older workers. They instituted flexible working and a retirement scheme to help older staff already in post, and ran recruitment campaigns aimed at the over-65s.

Sainsbury's has found the many benefits of its Age Positive policies include improved customer satisfaction "by more accurately reflecting the profile of customers," according to a spokesman. Latest available figures show that nearly 15% of employees are over 50 and 1.2% are over 65.

However much you might fancy the idea of casting aside your cares and rushing off to sign up with the happy armies of part-timers employed in superstores the length and breadth of the country, there are one or two cautionary points to bear in mind first.

They come from Matthew, a specialist work consultant to the over-55s, who finds he has to spell out the drawbacks and counsel caution time and again when faced with a highly paid executive or a top level PA eager to spend at least part of their retirement 'just stacking shelves'. The phrase, of course, covers a multitude of unskilled jobs, but it manages to convey some of the undemanding, repetitious nature of that sort of work.

"There are issues associated with working in, let's call it a routine job," Matthew says. "For some people it can be a lovely change, even for people from quite a senior level. They have the personal contact, they've got no real responsibilities at all, it gives them something to do, which is great if they haven't any outside interests, and it gives some sense of purpose and camaraderie. They're looked after. They come in, they do their job and they walk away.

"But I do get people to think about the other side to all that. I know about this because I was warned to be very careful myself, by a recruitment consultant, when I was wondering about doing some night-time shelf stacking for my local Tesco when I was made redundant 10 years ago. He said for some people it works very well but other people, particularly if they've had quite a responsible job in business, can find it difficult to make the change. They find it very frustrating because they go in and they start stacking shelves, say, and they start to think 'This is crazy, they shouldn't be doing it like this. There's a far better way than this. They've got six people here but they could make do with three.'

"There's also the fact that you're working with a different type of person – and I don't mean this to come across in the wrong way – but it is an issue. You sit down at lunchtime and they get out the *Sun* and are marking off all the horses for the afternoon's racing and you get out your *Guardian* or your *Telegraph* and there's a difference between you already.

"You might find yourself part of a team where there's quite a lot of fiddling ('Why don't we put this down on your sheet? Don't worry about it, and if you want a box of screws, too …') and if you are someone of quite a high integrity that can be very difficult.

"So for some people it works very well but for other people it doesn't. It's as well to be forewarned."

Matthew says he knows a number of people who have retired from quite a responsible job in industry to driving a taxi. "That works really well," he says. "A former work colleague of mine at senior level now runs an airport taxi service. It adds up to chunky bits of driving and you tend to get good tips."

> Taxi and private hire is a growing market – 32% of the public use a taxi at least once a month, compared to 16% in the mid-1980s. There are currently 500,000 private hire and taxi drivers in the UK. The private hire and taxi industry was worth £2.6 billion in 2005, so it could be a good move to try and take a share of that.
>
> You will need to apply to your local council for a private hire operator licence, for which you must prove that you are a 'fit and proper person'. The cost is likely to be about £300. The National Private Hire Association [0161 280 2800 www.privatehiretaximonthly.com/npha.html] represents more than 400 private hire firms. If you are thinking of becoming a taxi driver, contact your local council to find out the cost of a Certificate of Compliance/licence. The Licensed Taxi Drivers Association [020 7286 1046] will help.
>
> There is currently no compulsory training programme, although an Intermediate Certificate in Licence Education for Taxi and Private Hire exists to provide a nationally recognised qualification for drivers. Find out more from the Private Hire, Hackney Carriage and Chauffeur Training Organisation on 0191 296 0814.
>
> Your vehicle, which will need to be clean and immaculate at all times, is meant to have an MOT three times a year, and bear in mind that you are unlikely to get insurance for a car that is more than 10 years old.

"I know courier drivers as well," Matthew adds, "and people doing Tesco home delivery who are very enthusiastic about it.

"Only you can judge if it's worth all the effort for the money. Mind you, a delivery driver I know, who must be well into his 60s, almost always gets offered a cup of tea, is very often given a tip and, so far, has had three offers of sex."

Delivery jobs have other plus points, too: you're in charge of your own work and you're working on your own, so the business of mixing in with a team isn't relevant, you're meeting customers for a small part of the day, and, perhaps best and most attractive of all, when you've done the job it's done. There are very few jobs like that.

Little wonder that home delivery and taxi driving have become popular jobs among retirees.

The supermarket checkout operator

Noel, 73, formerly an accounting supervisor with BA

Why are you still working?

Being single I get bored on my own. I enjoy people's company, and of course the money helps.

What are you doing?

I work on the food checkout in Marks & Spencer. I am very much a people person and an extrovert and consequently I relate well to people. I work approximately 24 hours a week, between midday and 6.15pm.

How did it come about?

My niece and her family took me into care in Bristol after I'd had an emergency triple heart bypass operation. I was bored staying in the house so after a few months I joined M&S in Bristol, working on the food checkouts. I transferred back to London the following year.

Is it working out well for you?

It's working really well. I have the best of both worlds: I have my independence (I've lived alone in Swiss Cottage NW3 since I came to England in 1958) and I am able to go to my niece and her family in Bristol at least once a month for a long weekend.

And the money?

I earn about £600 a month, net. Despite the fact I trained to be a chartered accountant in London and failed the final examination twice (the last time at the age of 47), I handle my own self-assessment forms!

PROS:

- The money funds my lifestyle. I am able to go to the theatre, concerts, eat out, and, of course, travel with my free BA tickets
- I can afford to spoil my great-nieces and nephews both here and in Sri Lanka
- I am able to continue to subscribe monthly to World Vision to support young Daniel in Zambia

CONS:

- None at all

> Marks & Spencer pays all its 65,000 employees on the basis of their responsibility and their performance, not on their age. As 80% of the workforce is part-time, the company takes into account their wider responsibilities at various stages of their lives. Accordingly it gives options for, among other things, four weeks' paid dependency leave for carers and a nine-month unpaid dependency break for carers, many of whom are likely to be in the older age group.

> In 2001 Marks & Spencer dispensed with its mandatory retirement age of 65, allowing staff to go on working until they choose to retire. Since then, the number of employees aged over 65 has increased from 27 to more than 1,000 and the over-60s employee population has grown to 5% of the workforce.

The driver and babysitter

Penny, 66, formerly a preparatory school secretary

Why are you still working?

Partly for financial reasons and partly because I need to do something. A new headteacher at the prep school where I was working asked me to leave four years ago (I took him for unfair dismissal), otherwise I might have been there until I was 70.

What are you doing?

I drive for a woman who is partially sighted and has two children, aged nine and 11. They are taken either to the station or to school every day. I collect them from after-school events. I also take the mother to the shops, etc. She is able to do a lot on her own, but obviously nothing that involves driving. I also babysit for the family. I have recently reduced the number of days I work from five to three.

I also work very occasionally for a retired solicitor doing his typing and organising his dinner parties and other entertaining.

How did it come about?

The collection of the children came via a friend who ran an agency meeting children from airports. I worked for her when I could while still working as a school secretary. She had a stroke last year and I took over helping this particular family. The work with the solicitor came about through a friend who knew him.

Is it working out well for you?

Yes, for the moment.

And the money?

As I don't get paid in the school holidays it is difficult to know. I get roughly £800 a month but then this is only for about eight months. It is, I suppose, pocket money. It certainly pays for the odd cheap holiday and gives me a few extras. Otherwise I only have my pensions and a few small investments. I am not sure about the tax implications of earning a small amount like this – and I'm not enquiring.

PROS:

- It gets me out of the house
- I am very fond of the two girls I look after

CONS:

- None really, except the early start in the morning
- It is a tie in that I have to be available morning and afternoon, which is something I thought I had finished with when my children grew up

The exam invigilator

Margaret, 61, formerly a civil servant (principal officer grade) in the Department of Health

Why are you still working?

Interest, company, a commitment to education, cash.

What are you doing?

I am an examinations invigilator, both in secondary schools and at university. This is episodic but full-time work, available when there are exams (eg mock GCSEs in winter, university finals in May). I have also been a film extra. Otherwise, I spend my days doing historical research for my own interest, which is definitely unpaid labour.

How did it come about?

For the schools work I applied to Capita Education Resourcing [**www.capitaresourcing.org.uk** *primary schools: 0800 731 6871; secondary: 0800 731 6872; further education: 0800 316 1332; nursery, SEN & support staff: 0800 731 6873*]. For the university work I applied direct to Queen Mary College, London University. Both accepted me.

Is it working out well for you?

I enjoy many aspects of it. As I possess natural authority and am a good organiser I feel – and am – valued in this role, although the job itself is not wildly exciting or mentally challenging.

And the money?

The university pays me at senior invigilator (team leader) rate, which at the last count was £85 per day. Capita pays me according to the distance I have to travel to reach a school; it varies between £7.50 and £8.60 per hour. This augments my pensions and is really pocket money, though it provides for extras like holidays, renewal of household goods, outings, clothes, meals out and the like. And I have three companion cats with expensive food tastes.

I am free of National Insurance contributions but liable for income tax at 22%.

I don't earn enough, either in point of time or amount, to need an accountant. All tax from earnings is deducted at source.

PROS:
- The physical activity
- The camaraderie with colleagues, staff and students
- The contact with the education process

CONS:

- Not many; I am worth more, and am regularly tempted to apply for a permanent (academic) job, but I am still enjoying the respite from being tied to office hours

The dog walker

Richard, 62, formerly a partner in an advertising agency

Why are you still working?

I don't like being idle and I do like the idea of earning a bit of extra money. My wife is still working so this seemed like a good way for me to stay out of the pub.

What are you doing?

Walking dogs for owners who are out all day, and occasionally boarding dogs in our home – all on a very informal basis.

How did it come about?

It started with a doggy sleepover. Friends asked me if their labrador could come and stay for a weekend while they were away. Word spread and, before I knew it, I was hosting a succession of pooches, nearly all owned by friends or friends of friends.

Most spend only a few hours a day, while their owners are at work, but there is a regular flow of dogs – though never more than two at a time – bringing their baskets, cuddlies and favourite toys to stay a night or two.

All are taken out for regular walks, through parks, woodland, across fields and along pavements, depending on their habits and preferences.

Is it working out well for you?

It's good fun. It isn't a big money earner, to be honest, but it does give me some extra pocket money. I've met a huge variety of interesting people and some great dogs. Most of the dogs are terrier varieties, a breed that was unknown to me as I had always had spaniels and labradors, with the notable exception of Tootsie, our West Highland terrier.

I have now got involved in gundogs, too, and I'm hoping to develop this with training, thereby giving me outdoor exercise as well as something for the pot.

The dog walking has got me away from spending too long at the computer or sitting in the garden, pub, wine bar or whatever. The dog usually reminds me that it's walking time so there's no danger I'll sit around and grow fat.

All the owners are terrific – I've no complaints at all. It's a great little enterprise to be involved in because we all have a common interest and so I've made plenty of good friends. Fortunately they tell their friends, and so on, so I'm never short of doggy companions.

Because it's very informal, just a casual arrangement between me and the owners, no one worries about the sort of rules and regulations that govern, for example, a licensed kennels. It operates on mutual trust and common sense, with a large helping of empathy, which I consider vital.

And the money?

It trickles in. It won't make me rich, but it's enough to make the effort worthwhile and that's all that matters really.

The four-legged friends each pay £8 for a sleepover or an 8am–6pm stay, with at least one good walk included. All doggy habits, endearing or irritating, are catered for, and contentment comes at no extra cost.

PROS:

- Good for my health because it keeps me occupied and active

- It has the makings of a much more structured, profitable business if I wanted it to, especially once my wife stops work

- I don't feel guilty if I spend a little more than I should on a slap-up curry

CONS:

- It is a tie, a commitment that must be taken seriously. I undertake to care to the very best of my ability for someone else's dearly loved pet. If we're invited away at short notice we can't always take the dog(s) with us. However, we manage to get round the problem by careful planning

The estate agent's assistant

Pam, 66, formerly regional officer for a national charity

Why are you still working?

To keep me in shoes! Seriously, I need the money to maintain a reasonable standard of living. I came out of a divorce very badly from a financial point of view in my mid-50s and since then I've always known I'd have to work long beyond 'retirement'. I have a small mortgage that should be paid off by the time I'm 70 so that – and the need for shoes and more shoes, of course – will keep my nose to the grindstone.

What are you doing?

I work for five hours a day, four days a week as an office assistant for a firm of independent estate agents. I also accompany viewers around houses out of my normal working hours, including weekends.

The office work involves me in all sorts as I just get on with whatever needs doing. It could be anything from mailing out house details to writing confidential letters on behalf of the director, who is responsible for commercial properties.

The bits I like best are helping to match people to the right houses and dealing with the dozens of people who come into the office every day, for whatever reason. Some of them may be coming in to make an offer for a house they've been to view, and that's always exciting. I don't actually deal with that side of things, because that's the job of a negotiator, but I am involved in the liaison and deal with much of the paperwork.

How did it come about?

I answered an advertisement in the local paper. I didn't think I'd stand a chance of getting the job because of my age (I was 61 at the time) and because it was so many years since I'd last put together a CV and applied for a job, let alone had an interview.

Fortunately, they weren't the slightest bit interested in my age but were impressed by my background in office administration and my ability to get on with people. I think it may have helped that I bought my present house through them 10 years ago and we got on well at the time, but perhaps I'm kidding myself.

Is it working out well for you?

It's wonderful. I am very happy. I enjoy working with such a good crowd of people and being made to feel not just useful but indispensable. I'm the oldest employee so I'm the sort of granny figure, but I don't mind that. I don't have children or grandchildren of my own, so I suppose they're my sort of family. We have a lot of fun and laughs. It's a very good place to work.

And the money?

For the time I put in and for the commitment I think I'm very poorly paid, but for the actual skills required it isn't too bad. It's £7 an hour, which is the equivalent of about £14,000 a year – probably the going rate for an office assistant in the provinces.

For the house viewing I get £6.50 an hour plus expenses of 40p a mile.

When I'm showing people a freezing cold house at 5pm on a dark Saturday evening I remind myself that it's no good complaining and I'm lucky to have the job. I have had a couple of pay rises in the five years I've been with the firm, so maybe there's another one round the corner.

I call to mind what my ex-husband always said, too: that if you're earning money at least you're not out spending it.

PROS:

- Meeting people and making friends
- Getting to know the area and what makes it tick
- Indulging my interest in houses
- Keeping active physically and mentally
- The money – it makes quite a difference
- Making me a more interesting person to talk to

CONS:

- I get quite tired sometimes, especially if I do my five hours at the office and then a couple of viewings
- It can be very disruptive if I'm called out at short notice to do a viewing (although this doesn't happen very often)
- The commitment – it is considerable and means I can't plan too far ahead in case I'm needed for viewings. I can say no, but I like to be reliable – and I like the money!

- Having to pay tax, which I really resent, but I like to keep everything above board

The hospital car driver

Bob, 68, formerly a county mobile librarian

Why are you still working?

For lots of reasons but the three main ones are to meet people, to keep out from under my wife's feet, and to keep busy and useful.

What are you doing?

I work five eight-hour days a week as a driver for the hospital car service. This means I could be travelling 130 miles taking a patient to London for a serious operation or someone to the local clinic for an outpatient's appointment. I take all sorts, at all times of the day and night. I once had to take a man to one of the London hospitals for a 7am operation and the police stopped me and asked me what I was doing at 4.30 in the morning. They'd just patrolled past my house and seen my car there, so were suspicious that it was suddenly on the move through town at such an unearthly hour. They were very surprised when I explained where I was going.

The work isn't difficult or particularly taxing, but you have to know your way round hospital sites and try and second-guess the people who devised the signage, which often leaves a lot to be desired.

I have a modest-sized people carrier, so there's plenty of room for the people I have to transport, unless they're in a wheelchair, in which case they have to go by ambulance.

How did it come about?

I had to retire early – I was only 53 – on health grounds. I'd had a heart attack and of course I couldn't go on driving the library bus or continue with my weekend job of driving a coach. Being responsible for HGVs and what was inside them was definitely not allowed at that stage. After a year of recovering I told my doctor that I felt as though I was on the scrapheap.

He disagreed and told me he knew just the job for me. It turned out to be for the hospital car service, which really appealed to me because I wanted to be helpful and before my heart attack I'd been a volunteer driver of the Multiple Sclerosis bus. I filled in the hospital car service forms on the Friday and started work on the Monday. They were that desperate!

Is it working out well for you?

Yes, I love it. I am raring to go in the mornings – I can't wait for the day to start. I never get bored, there isn't time for that, and I always enjoy meeting the patients. It's so nice doing something useful.

And the money?

The hospital car service is a non-profit making organisation and the drivers are all volunteers. However, it is possible to profit a little from the allowances I receive. For example, after covering my expenses, which include car tax, insurance, petrol and depreciation, I probably clear about £5,000 a year. For a five-day-a-week commitment with quite a bit of responsibility this isn't much, to be honest, but it's not something you would do if you were anxious to make a lot of money.

Having said that, it does make all the difference between us being able to afford to buy something and not. My wife and I don't have to worry if we want anything, we just buy it because we know we've got that bit extra behind us.

PROS:

• Meeting people

• Working with the public, which I love

- Filling a useful role in the community
- Getting out from under my wife's feet

CONS:

- Having to go out early when the weather is bad
- Coping with a few grumpy people in the control centre who don't know where they're sending you half the time

The cleaning lady

Betty, 72, formerly a shop assistant

Why are you still working?

For the money, of course. My husband died quite young when I was in my mid-50s so I had a pretty tough time making ends meet. I'm not the sort who'd sit around not doing much – my life would be so miserable if I did that. My pensions and benefits would just about keep me ticking along but I'd have to go without all life's pleasures, so while I can still turn my hand to a bit of work, I will do.

What are you doing?

I do cleaning work. I pick and choose who I work for and I avoid anything that looks too physically demanding because my back plays me up. I've got dodgy knees, too.

I do a couple of hours most mornings for decent people who live fairly close to me. I don't have transport – I have never driven a car and I can't ride my bicycle any more – so it has to be close enough for me to walk to my jobs. If I had to pay bus fares, it wouldn't be worth it.

I work on a regular weekly basis in four people's houses, two hours in three of them, three hours in the other, and I do Sunday mornings for the couple who run the local pub. They live above the pub and I clean for them. It's nice because I get to see their children. Sometimes I stay on and have lunch with them, and that's lovely. Sundays would be awful without this job to go to. I have my Saturdays free, so that's when I go to my daughter's.

How did it come about?

I got the first job, the one that's for three hours, by answering an advert in the newsagent's window. The other jobs came about through that one – word of mouth, I suppose.

Is it working out well for you?

Yes, I think so. I just hope my health holds out because sometimes I find it quite exhausting. Everyone I work for is very understanding and they don't mind if I work at my own pace.

And the money?

I earn just under £100 most weeks, which may not seem a lot to many people but it is to me. It makes all the difference in the world. It's not taxed – I'm paid in cash.

PROS:

- Having some money in my purse for the little things and for going out
- I like all the people I work for
- It keeps me busy
- There's nearly always someone around to have a chat with

CONS:

- It can be hard work for the money
- I worry about how I'll manage when I just can't do it any more

The house sitter

Miriam, 64, formerly full-time food writer and editor (now part-time)

Why are you still working?

For the money.

What are you doing?

I look after people's houses, gardens/grounds and their animals while they are away.

It involves living in and dealing with pretty much everything that country life can throw at you. For example, I've had a dead sheep, literally, on my hands. "Just find a knacker," the owner bellowed at me down the phone.

Then there are dogs that like to wander; a dog that has epileptic fits every half-hour or so for several hours and the vet being unobtainable; dealing with an insulin dependent dog that started to go into shock several times (due to lack of information from the owners); an intruder who came back three times, claiming that he owned the extensive manor house containing antique silver, valuable paintings and even a designer ironing board; a flooded cellar; a complicated, labour intensive connection of a generator during an extended power cut; a fox in with the chickens.

Agencies will specify that you should not be away from the house for more than three or four hours at a time during the day and not at all at night.

How did it come about?

I saw advertisements for house sitting in magazines. It appealed because I live alone and can easily close up my house at short notice if necessary.

Is it working out well for you?

It has done for the eight years I've been doing it, but I'm beginning to feel I've had enough of being away so much.

And the money?

It really is no more than pin money. Agencies warn that it can only be seen as a secondary source of income, which is why so many pensioners do it.

PROS:

- A bit of money

- Provides opportunities to see other parts of the general area in which you live, although the cost of travel precludes going too far afield

- I like getting out and about, especially in winter, which I loathe, so I particularly appreciate having somewhere different to go during those months

- I like having animals to look after. Some people might not, and that would mean less money if you do just house-sitting

- Some saving on my own utility bills but not as much as you might think because I have to leave my fridge and freezer running at home as well as some heat in winter and lights on time switches

CONS:

- If you use an agency, they will take some of your money, in some way

- If you 'sit' for friends you might not be able to charge as much – I've found most people, even when very well off, baulk at paying anywhere near the going rate

- If you need a particularly comfortable mattress, it's not for you – you never know what you'll get

- If you like seeing friends and neighbours or anyone on a regular basis, forget it. Many places are deep in the country, especially where animals are involved

- It can be pointless joining clubs or signing up for evening classes because you can never know if you're going to be at home or away

- You might not be told all an animal's bad traits

- You have to be prepared to deal with emergencies in connection with animals and house

- My own home and garden are left unattended a lot

- Being responsible for someone's animals and their house means it is not a very relaxing way of life

The arts reviewer

Leslie, 84, formerly a small-business owner in a provincial town

Why are you still working?

It was really a means of getting to know people. I didn't sell the business until I was 75 but then my wife and I moved to another town to be closer to our children and grandchildren. Obviously we knew no one else here and we realised that the best way to meet new people and find our way around was to get involved in the life of the place in some way. The fact that this turned out to be through work for which I get paid was just a happy coincidence.

What are you doing?

I work as an arts reviewer for three newspapers – two local weeklies, one regional daily. My specialist knowledge of various types of music, particularly jazz, but also classical, goes back 60 years or more to the days when I played in a jazz band; my knowledge of the theatre and art is less comprehensive or indeed expert but I had a 'proper' education so have always had a facility with words and language.

The amount of time I spend reviewing varies according to the time of year. During our local arts festival, for example, I may be out every night for two weeks or more, as well as some daytime outings to art exhibitions and the like. Then of course I have to get everything written up and submitted, which I do via email.

I probably go out for a minimum of two evenings a month and a maximum of six. It is hard to calculate the number of hours I do in a year but if I don't like the sound of a particular event or if I'm just not feeling up to it, then I can always decline the commission.

How did it come about?

My son and my daughter are both journalists and were able to recommend me for the work to the editors and arts editors of newspapers where they either work or have worked. I've never been daunted by taking on a new challenge and this has been something so completely different from anything that I've ever done before that it certainly comes under that heading.

Is it working out well for you?

Yes, I enjoy it very much, although sometimes it can be a little tiring. But it has fulfilled all my hopes: my wife and I have learnt a lot about our new home town, made a lot of new friends and acquaintances, seen and heard some truly thrilling live music, and made a few extra pounds which has been great for my morale. I didn't take up this work until I was 80, so it is lovely to think I can still do something useful and do it well enough to be paid even at my stage in life.

And the money?

It's not a fortune – local newspapers don't pay like *The Sun*, I'm afraid. But all totalled up, I'd guess it's maybe a couple of thousand pounds a year. It doesn't make a great difference, to be honest, because our needs are fairly few, but it all goes into the pot and when we need to buy something – such as having the computer repaired or upgraded or replacing the TV or the fridge, it's nice to think that something so highly enjoyable has paid for it.

Because I'm only earning what amounts to pocket money I'm sure the taxman isn't the slightest bit interested in me. Ignorance is bliss, on both sides.

PROS:

- The extra money
- A revived sense of one's own worth
- The opportunity to meet new people, visit new places, hear, see and be part of a lively arts scene
- Staying in touch with the modern world
- Having something interesting to talk about with the family and with others that doesn't revolve around the problems of old age

CONS:

- Sometimes – rarely but sometimes – I'd rather slump in an arm-chair in front of the television in my old comfortable clothes instead of having to wash and shave and change and go out, especially on a wet winter night
- Once in a while I see a dreadful play or a third rate art exhibition and it can be a struggle to find the right words to express my feelings without crushing the enthusiasm of those who have staged it. I am conscious of the responsibility I have in this direction
- I don't know how much longer my health and stamina will allow me to keep working; also I am almost totally dependant on my wife to drive me to assignments as I have stopped driving now

and she is quite a lot younger than me. The down side is that she has to come with me to every event and sometimes she is less enthusiastic than I am

The exercise class tutor

Pat, 85, formerly headteacher of a special school

Why are you still working?

To ensure I remain active and interested in life. It's also a small way of putting something back into the community which I love. I retired to this house in the county of my birth after my husband died and while I am fortunate to have my health I shall continue to work for other people's benefit.

What are you doing?

I teach Extend classes to people aged 60 and over. Extend is a sequence of exercises and movement to music designed to keep older people fit and help the less mobile become more supple and balanced [wwwextend.org.uk 01582 832760].

For the past 19 years I have been running Extend classes in my home town. The largest class, with 32 on the roll, is in a church hall and I also run classes in three retirement homes.

The class in the hall is meant to last for an hour but we always over-run because we enjoy ourselves so much. We're like a big group of friends. Every summer I have an open day in my garden and all the class members come and have lunch and we organise a raffle, a cake stall and various games to raise money for the national headquarters of Extend.

How did it come about?

I went to Women's League of Health and Beauty classes when I lived and worked in London and through my membership of that I went to a physical fitness exhibition in Olympia. It was there that I was fascinated to discover that Extend exercises were a modified version of these, and very similar in principle, but aimed at older people. So after I retired from work I trained as an Extend teacher. My tutor was Seona Ross, who is now in her 90s and still teaching.

It is such a good qualification to have because you can take it with you wherever you go, although obviously you have to stay up to date through refresher courses.

Is it working out well for you?

It's wonderful. It gives me all I could wish for and more. Along with the charity work I do for the lifeboats, it keeps me occupied and active.

And the money?

Incomes are very low in my region so I only make a nominal charge for my classes. I couldn't charge any more or I'd feel bad. So many of the people who come to my class in the church hall are on small pensions and I wouldn't want to deny them the chance of coming to Extend. They pay me £1 for the hour-long class, but that was only after they'd convinced me I ought to put it up from 50p and then 75p.

The hall costs £5 an hour, but I fear that will be going up soon, which could be a problem.

The retirement homes pay me £20 an hour. I don't earn very much from being an Extend teacher, but that isn't why I do it. If I organised more classes I could earn more, and some Extend teachers earn a considerable amount more, but this is how I like it.

PROS:

• I'm doing something I really enjoy

- It keeps me fit and occupied
- The people are lovely
- It is of benefit to the community

CONS:

- I can't think of a single one

Chapter 11

Over to you

If this book has given you pause for thought then it has succeeded. My hope – and intention – is that it should be a source of inspiration, a springboard to set you off on a new phase of life.

I have endeavoured to maintain a sense of objectivity as I have related the many varied journeys on which some retirees have embarked, yet if there is one overriding lesson that I would like to pass on it is this: there are innumerable good reasons for people to work in their retirement and earning extra money is only one of them.

Therefore, if money does happen to be your one and only motivation you will, I am sure, be rewarded and enriched in many other ways.

The tax situation

An important area of concern for anyone thinking of earning money in their retirement is the situation regarding tax. Current guidelines and information on allowances for earners and tax payers of all ages are available on the *Earning Money After You've Retired* page of the White Ladder Press website: **www.whiteladderpress.com**.

Alternatively, if you are close to 60 or older and your household income is less than £15,000, you can get excellent advice from the Tax Help for Older People (TOP) **www.taxvol.org.uk helpline 0845 601 3321**.

Information

Here are some sources of help and/or inspiration for anyone seeking information on working post-retirement. You can also find these on our website at **www.whiteladderpress.com**.

www.agepositive.gov.uk – the campaign that promotes the benefits of employing a mixed-age workforce

www.efa.org.uk – tackles ageism at work

www.fiftyon.co.uk – information on ageism, employment, lifestyle, offers and discounts

www.heyday.org.uk – information and opportunities "to maximise the quality of life"

www.hmrc.gov.uk – all you need to know about HM Revenue & Customs

www.inmyprime.co.uk – information and inspiration "for mature, positive, energetic people who want to achieve more"

www.laterlife.com – web magazine that aims to maximise enjoyment for over-50s and help them "live life to the full"

www.life-academy.co.uk – advice on "preparing for life's next steps" (formerly the Pre-Retirement Association)

www.over50.gov.uk – everything from benefits to well-being and from learning to earning

www.primeinitiative.org.uk – specifically to help over-50s set up in business

www.saga.co.uk – website of the over-50s' Saga magazine with advice, information, features and offers

www.taen.org.uk – experts in age and employment

Useful contacts

You'll find all the websites referred to in this book on our website at **www.whiteladderpress.com** to make it easier for you to access them. Click on 'Useful contacts' next to the information about this book.

Contact us

You're welcome to contact White Ladder Press if you have any questions or comments for either us or the author. Please use whichever of the following routes suits you.

Phone 01803 813343 between 9am and 5.30pm

Email enquiries@whiteladderpress.com

Fax 01803 813928

Address White Ladder Press, Great Ambrook, Near Ipplepen, Devon TQ12 5UL

Website www.whiteladderpress.com

What can our website do for you?

If you want more information about any of our books, you'll find it at **www.whiteladderpress.com**. In particular you'll find extracts from each of our books, and reviews of those that are already published. We also run special offers on future titles if you order online before publication. And you can request a copy of our free catalogue.

Many of our books also have links pages, useful addresses and so on relevant to the subject of the book. You'll also find out a bit more about us and, if you're a writer yourself, you'll find our submission guidelines for authors. So please check us out and let us know if you have any comments, questions or suggestions.

"Spot-on, thought provoking, and often very funny. So you think you already know how to suck eggs? Let this frisky, friendly 'how-to' book tell you how to do it better and enjoy it more!" **Irma Kurtz**

The Insider's Guide to Being a Brilliant Grandparent

It's so exciting finding out you're about to become a grandparent. But it can be a bit scary too. After all, it has its share of potential pitfalls. Many expectant and new grandparents are nervous at how they'll cope with the new role, and want to know how other grandparents have managed to make the relationship – with their children as well as their grandchildren – as rewarding as possible.

That's why grandfather of seven Phill Williams has written *The Insider's Guide to Being a Brilliant Grandparent*. Based on a survey of grandparents, and interviews with grandchildren, this is a practical and readable guide to all the joys and challenges new grandparents face, including:

- What to do if you disagree with how your children look after your grandchildren
- Babysitting your grandchildren
- Getting on with the other grandparents
- Choosing presents
- Going on holiday together
- Long distance grandparenting
- Step-grandchildren
- Coping with divorced families
- Having the grandchildren to stay

...and plenty more

This essential guide is packed with the cumulative wisdom, advice and support of grandparents from every walk of life, pulled together in one place so you can get on and enjoy your growing family.   £7.99

Also by Rosie Staal

"The book manages to be three things all at the same time, which is very remarkable. It is readable, humorous and extremely informative." CLAIRE RAYNER

What shall we do with Mother?

What to do when your elderly parent is dependent on you

All your life your parents have been capable adults, looking after themselves and, indeed, looking after you when you needed it.

And then you start to notice – often after your other parent's death – that your mum or dad is beginning to flounder. Maybe their health is starting to go or, frighteningly, their mind.

What Shall We Do With Mother? tells the stories of six people in just your situation, each struggling to care for a mother or father who increasingly needs their help. It passes on their experience, mistakes and advice for coping with:

- the dilemma of whether to put them in a home
- family pressures and conflicting demands on your time
- balancing what's best for them with what's best for you
- parents who develop difficult personalities or dementia
- the inevitable guilt that besets everyone in your position

Above all, their stories reassure you that you're not alone and there is a way through, to give your mum or dad the support they need without having to sacrifice your own sanity.

£9.99

OUT OF YOUR TOWNIE MIND

THE REALITY BEHIND THE DREAM OF COUNTRY LIVING

"Richard Craze yanks the rose-tinted spectacles from the rural idyll and tramples them in the mud. The result is cheeky but charming — a kind of Feel-the-Fear-But-Do-It-Anyway for wannabe downshifters." **Hugh Fearnley-Whittingstall**

We all have our own fantasy of what life in the country will be like. But are we right? Is it all roses round the door, or are they really brambles?

So you're finally sick of city life. You close your eyes and dream of living in the country — all that space, and wonderful views. Going for long walks and coming home to an open fire, bringing your children up healthy and safe and being part of a community. Maybe you have visions of baking cakes on an Aga, keeping your own hens and handknitting your own yoghurt...

But will it really be like that?

Out of Your Townie Mind takes the most popular dreams of rural life that townies have (based on a survey of aspiring country dwellers) and lays the real facts on the line. Does a big garden really give you more space to enjoy the country, or just create so much work you never have time to enjoy it? Will a house in the woods be a private haven of wildlife, your own nature reserve on the doorstep... or is it just dark, damp and a recipe for endless gutter clearing?

Out of Your Townie Mind shows you how, with a bit of forethought, you can get the very best out of country living by avoiding the pitfalls other townies stumble into.

£7.99